Back Roads &
Hidden Corners

EXPLORE AMERICA

Back Roads & Hidden Corners

Reader's Digest

THE READER'S DIGEST ASSOCIATION, INC.
Pleasantville, New York / Montreal

BACK ROADS & HIDDEN CORNERS was created and produced by St. Remy Press.

PRESIDENT: Pierre Léveillé
PUBLISHER: Kenneth Winchester

STAFF FOR BACK ROADS & HIDDEN CORNERS
Series Editor: Carolyn Jackson
Series Art Director: Diane Denoncourt
Senior Editor: Elizabeth Cameron
Picture Editor: Christopher Jackson
Assistant Editor: Alfred LeMaitre
Researcher: Rory Gilsenan
Contributing Researcher: Olga Dzatko
Designer: Hélène Dion
Cartographer: Maryo Proulx
Index: Christine Jacobs

Writers: Bob Devine—Mendocino County, The Wallowas
Jim Henderson—Cajun Country, Texas Hill Country
Martin Hintz—Hidden Valleys
Rose Houk—San Juan Sojourn
Rick Marsi—Finger Lakes, Northeast Kingdom
James S. Wamsley—The Chesapeake, Potomac Highlands

Contributing Writers: Tracey Arial, Joanna Ebbutt,
Nancy Lyon, Victoria Ross, Bryce Walker

Administrator: Natalie Watanabe
Production Manager: Michelle Turbide
Systems Coordinator: Jean-Luc Roy

READER'S DIGEST STAFF
Editor: Fred DuBose
Art Director: Evelyn Bauer
Art Associate: Martha Grossman

READER'S DIGEST GENERAL BOOKS
Editor in Chief: John A. Pope, Jr.
Managing Editor: Jane Polley
Executive Editor: Susan J. Wernert
Art Director: David Trooper
Group Editors: Will Bradbury, Sally French,
Norman B. Mack, Kaari Ward
Group Art Editors: Evelyn Bauer,
Robert M. Grant, Joel Musler
Chief of Research: Laurel A. Gilbride
Copy Chief: Edward W. Atkinson
Picture Editor: Richard Pasqual
Rights and Permissions: Pat Colomban
Head Librarian: Jo Manning

Opening photographs
Cover: Countryside in autumn, Vermont
Back Cover: Town of Mendocino, California
Page 2: San Juan Mountains near Telluride, Colorado
*Page 5: Vineyards in Boonville, Mendocino
County, California*

The credits and acknowledgments that appear on page 144 are hereby made a part of this copyright page.

Library of Congress Cataloging in Publication Data

Back roads & hidden corners.
        p.   cm.—(Explore America)
    Includes index.
    ISBN 0-89577-545-X
    1. United States—Tours. 2. United States—Pictorial works.
    3. United States—Geography. I. Reader's Digest Association.
    II. Title: Back roads and hidden corners. III. Series
    E158.B124   1993
    917.304'929—dc20   93-8254

Printed in the United States of America
Second Printing, November 1995

CONTENTS

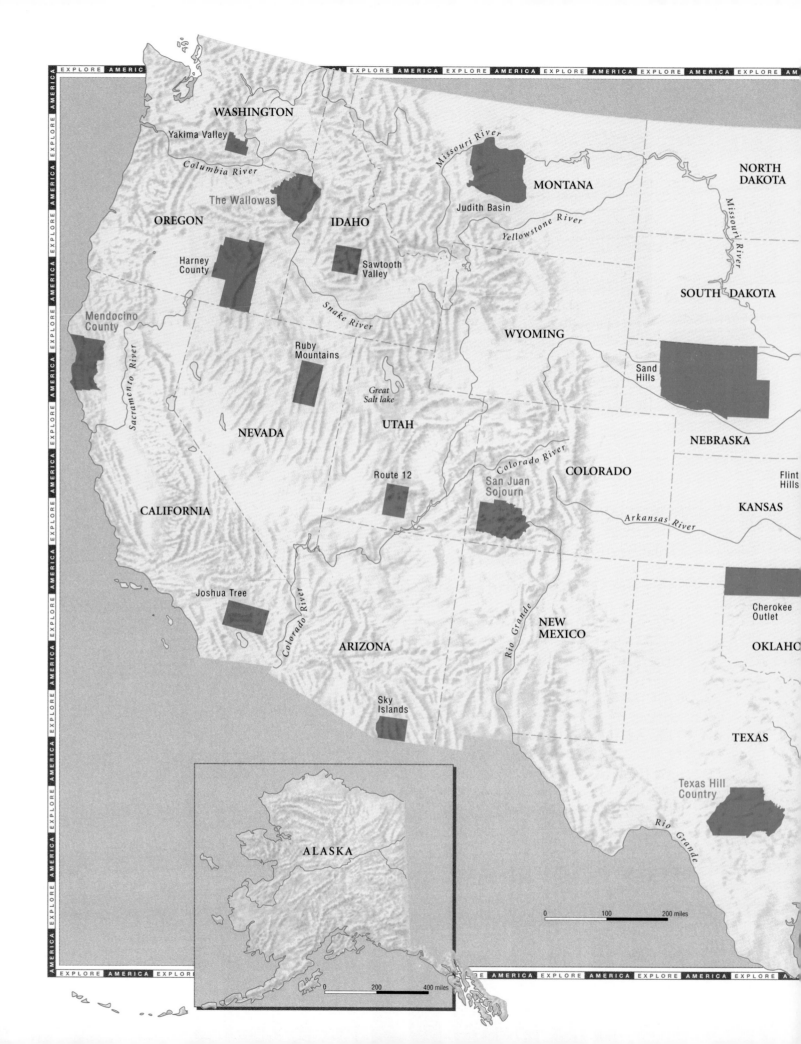

WASHINGTON

Yakima Valley

Columbia River

NORTH
DAKOTA

Missouri River

MONTANA

The Wallowas

Judith Basin

Yellowstone River

OREGON

IDAHO

Missouri River

Harney
County

Sawtooth
Valley

SOUTH DAKOTA

Snake River

Mendocino
County

WYOMING

Ruby
Mountains

Sacramento River

*Great
Salt lake*

Sand
Hills

NEVADA

UTAH

NEBRASKA

Route 12

Colorado River

COLORADO

Flint
Hills

San Juan
Sojourn

CALIFORNIA

KANSAS

Arkansas River

Cherokee
Outlet

Joshua Tree

Colorado River

NEW
MEXICO

Rio Grande

OKLAHO

ARIZONA

Sky
Islands

TEXAS

Texas Hill
Country

Rio Grande

ALASKA

0   100   200 miles

0   200   400 miles

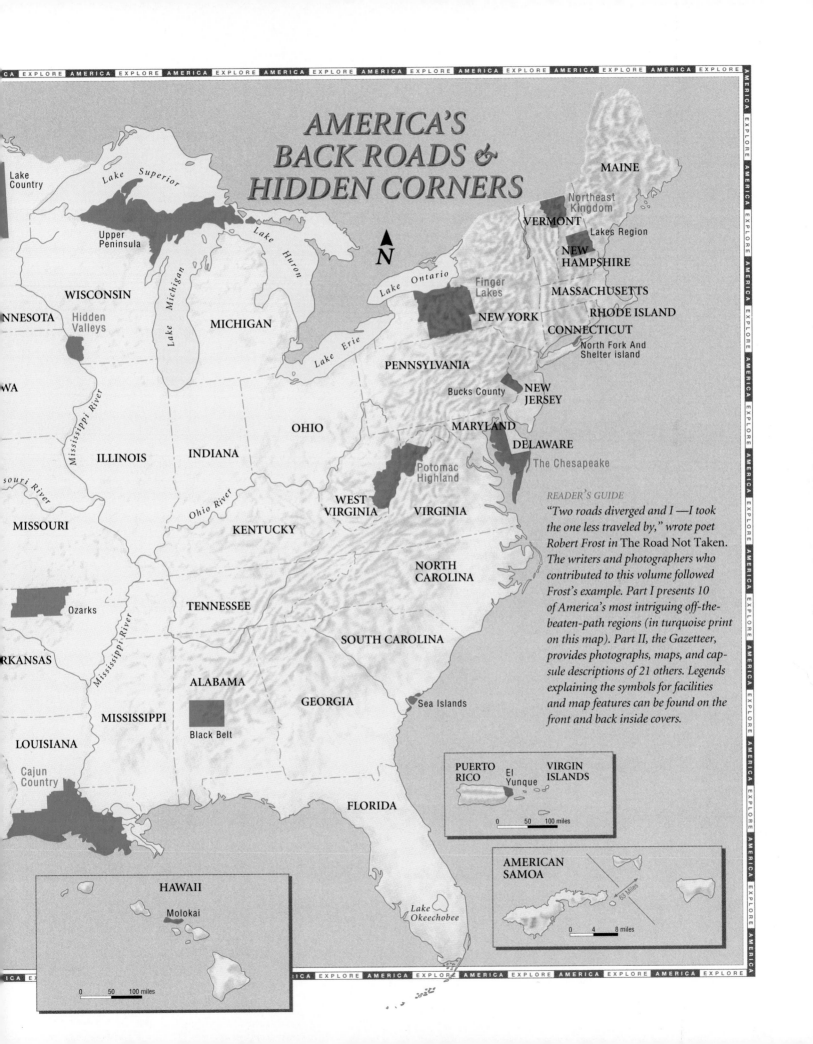

AMERICA'S BACK ROADS & HIDDEN CORNERS

READER'S GUIDE

"Two roads diverged and I —I took the one less traveled by," wrote poet Robert Frost in The Road Not Taken. The writers and photographers who contributed to this volume followed Frost's example. Part I presents 10 of America's most intriguing off-the-beaten-path regions (in turquoise print on this map). Part II, the Gazetteer, provides photographs, maps, and capsule descriptions of 21 others. Legends explaining the symbols for facilities and map features can be found on the front and back inside covers.

MAINE

Northeast Kingdom

VERMONT

Lakes Region

NEW HAMPSHIRE

MASSACHUSETTS

RHODE ISLAND

CONNECTICUT

North Fork And Shelter island

Finger Lakes

NEW YORK

Lake Ontario

Lake Country

Lake Superior

Upper Peninsula

Lake Huron

Lake Michigan

WISCONSIN

MINNESOTA

Hidden Valleys

MICHIGAN

IOWA

Mississippi River

Missouri River

MISSOURI

ILLINOIS

INDIANA

OHIO

Lake Erie

PENNSYLVANIA

Bucks County

NEW JERSEY

MARYLAND

DELAWARE

The Chesapeake

Potomac Highland

WEST VIRGINIA

VIRGINIA

KENTUCKY

ARKANSAS

Ozarks

Mississippi River

TENNESSEE

NORTH CAROLINA

SOUTH CAROLINA

ALABAMA

GEORGIA

Sea Islands

MISSISSIPPI

Black Belt

LOUISIANA

Cajun Country

FLORIDA

Lake Okeechobee

PUERTO RICO   El Yunque   VIRGIN ISLANDS

0   50   100 miles

AMERICAN SAMOA

63 Miles

0   4   8 miles

HAWAII

Molokai

0   50   100 miles

NORTHEAST KINGDOM

In this hidden corner of New England, the land and its climate impose daily guidelines for living.

Encompassing roughly 2,000 square miles in Vermont's northeastern corner, the "Kingdom" hasn't changed radically since Vermont Senator George Aiken coined the term in the 1940's. Singled out by Aiken for its fiercely independent people and unspoiled environs, this remote region still boasts more spruce trees than people, more forest than farmland and a year-round contingent of hardy Vermonters who know what a long winter means.

If "kingdom" connotes a world slightly set apart, or removed, then this place qualifies. Covering Essex, Orleans and Caledonia Counties, Vermont's least-populated region finds itself not only isolated by nature but by political boundaries. The Canadian border curtails the Kingdom's northward expansion; the Green Mountains loom to the west. Drive eastward too far, and you'll run out of state where the Connecticut River forms Vermont's boundary with New Hampshire.

Wherever you drive in the Northeast Kingdom, rest assured you won't bog down in traffic. The

There's no mistaking this landscape. It is quintessential Northeast Kingdom, with its signature steeple, red barn and grazing black and white Holsteins. The first blush of autumn only serves to heighten the simple, clean lines of Peacham's church spire as it rises over the rolling countryside.

Overleaf: Autumn paints the rolling fields of Cabot, Vermont. The town is known for its award-winning cheddar, produced by a cooperative creamery founded by dairy farmers in 1919.

region's one major highway, Interstate 91, is busy in summer and fall, but during other seasons its rest areas stand empty for long moments. During these interludes, bird songs, not car sounds, prevail.

Leave the interstate—and this holds true for any exit, from the Northeast Kingdom's southern gateway at St. Johnsbury to the Canadian border at Derby Line, 50 miles farther north—and you'll sense you have entered a place where the land and its people have learned to adapt to each other.

Back roads abound in the region, crisscrossing the rugged terrain in a lattice of blacktop and dirt. No matter what road you choose, if you drive for an hour, you'll see how this harmony works.

Chances are the road you've chosen will seek out a valley that snakes between forested hills. If you called these hills mountains, Montanans would laugh. Chances are, Floridians wouldn't. Thickly covered with birch, maple, spruce and white pine, the hills climb steeply enough to make casual strollers think twice. Yet they don't deny access to loggers who work their pitched slopes, dragging logs down rough trails to be stacked by the road.

Many back roads in the Kingdom feature farms intermingled with forest. Most of the farmsteads are modest in size. Many have been owned by the same family for generations. Thanks to their parents and grandparents, who paid off mortgages and other debts, a number of the region's current farmers own their places outright. They are the first to admit that without help from their predecessors, they wouldn't be able to stay on as small dairy farmers.

Many farms in the Kingdom are anchored by neat white farmhouses, tidy red barns and a modest contingent of Holstein and Jersey cows. Surrounding the buildings are crop fields that bear little resemblance to limitless Midwest expanses. Fall asleep for three seconds while you are plowing a Northeast Kingdom cornfield, and you may slide right off into a brook.

That's because fields in the Kingdom refuse to lie flat. They pitch and roll, squeezed between a road or stream on one side and a wooded hillside on the other. What the fields lack in flatness, they make up for in rocks. Most of the rocks have been picked from the fields and piled into cobblestone walls. Occasionally, a huge boulder stands out in a field's very center. Half-buried and immovable, it confirms that nature can't be pushed very far in Vermont. Plow around the big rocks; bend where nature says bend—that's a credo here.

POSTCARD-PERFECT VILLAGES

Turn a corner in the road, and a farm field gives way to a village. Most of the villages in the Kingdom seem to have jumped off the face of a postcard. Some lie tucked into hollows, others cling to side slopes or command gorgeous views from hilltop vantage points. Perfectly proportioned, they appear grafted to the landscape. Their white clapboard houses and soaring white steeples seem designed to highlight both the rolling landscape and the good sense of those who have chosen to make it their home. Take Peacham, for example, a

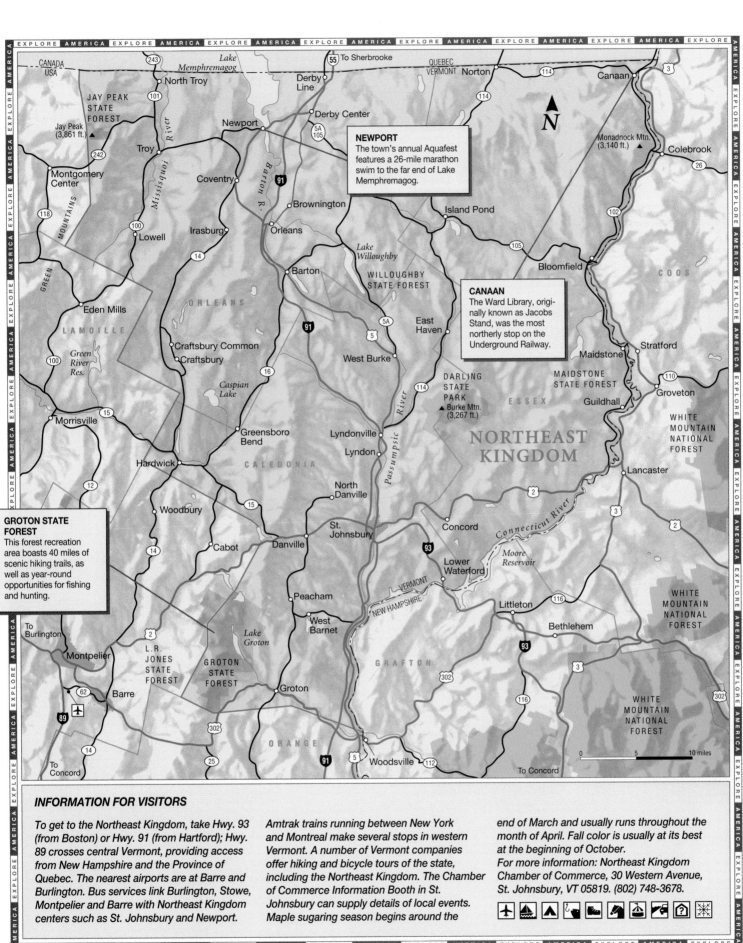

NEWPORT

The town's annual Aquafest features a 26-mile marathon swim to the far end of Lake Memphremagog.

CANAAN

The Ward Library, originally known as Jacobs Stand, was the most northerly stop on the Underground Railway.

GROTON STATE FOREST

This forest recreation area boasts 40 miles of scenic hiking trails, as well as year-round opportunities for fishing and hunting.

INFORMATION FOR VISITORS

To get to the Northeast Kingdom, take Hwy. 93 (from Boston) or Hwy. 91 (from Hartford); Hwy. 89 crosses central Vermont, providing access from New Hampshire and the Province of Quebec. The nearest airports are at Barre and Burlington. Bus services link Burlington, Stowe, Montpelier and Barre with Northeast Kingdom centers such as St. Johnsbury and Newport.

Amtrak trains running between New York and Montreal make several stops in western Vermont. A number of Vermont companies offer hiking and bicycle tours of the state, including the Northeast Kingdom. The Chamber of Commerce Information Booth in St. Johnsbury can supply details of local events. Maple sugaring season begins around the

end of March and usually runs throughout the month of April. Fall color is usually at its best at the beginning of October.

For more information: Northeast Kingdom Chamber of Commerce, 30 Western Avenue, St. Johnsbury, VT 05819. (802) 748-3678.

*DISTINCTIVE ARCHITECTURE
All roads lead to barns, it seems,
but not all barns look the same.
The circular barn, below, on Round
Barn Farm in East Barnet was
built—and built to last—in 1899.
The farm's old gas pump seems to
stand guard. At right, a covered
bridge near Coventry offers a vista
of a more traditional barn.*

little village south of St. Johnsbury. Girt by maple groves, Peacham's white houses and clapboard Congregational Church could almost be the model for many of the Kingdom's village jewels.

Aside from the steeples, few village buildings climb beyond two or three stories. When the wind blows in winter, Vermonters live close to the ground. Cold weather does set the Kingdom apart from more southerly sections of New England. Because winter comes early and departs at its leisure, other seasons spin by all too quickly. One minute it's mud season—March—when hard maples ooze sap and the sugarhouse stovepipes puff white steam in the air. The next, buds are bursting as spring paints steep hillsides a pale yel-

low-green with newly emerging leaves. Brief summer follows—lush hayfields, blue lakes, chilly nights and community picnics. Then it's autumn, with foliage flaming and stacked rows of firewood stretching the length of backyards.

In a wink, winter's back. That's not bad in this place. Cross-country skiers can slide through high fields, then across village commons where church bells play carols at Christmas.

| DIVERSITY MEANS SURVIVAL | Inured to the quickness with which the seasons change, the residents of the Northeast Kingdom have learned to embrace whatever the weath- |

er hands out with a blend of good humor and grit.

On the job front, a number of people have gritted their teeth and adapted. They've diversified, changing jobs with the seasons, finding work that will keep the bills paid. "Baked goods, barber shop, maple syrup," reads a sign by a log cabin near Island Pond in westernmost Essex County. If you asked, they could probably put you up for the night and sell you some firewood, too. In winter, Northeast Kingdom residents cater to cross-country and downhill skiers. The region's biggest downhill area, Jay Peak, boasts the highest average annual snowfall of any ski area east of the Rocky Mountains—300 inches. Outside Craftsbury Common, a hilltop village named for its founder, Ebenezer Crafts, the Craftsbury Nordic Ski Center offers some 70 miles of cross-country trails. To accommodate skiers, inns and bed-and-breakfasts pop up on back roads throughout the region. The Inn on the Common in Craftsbury Common entices prospective guests with this scintillating promise: If you put on your skis at the door of the inn, ski two miles through fields and forests to the Nordic Ski Center, you'll then be able to join its system of excellent trails.

Most of the signs in front of inns like the Inn on the Common are small and tastefully painted. Yet, they stand out boldly. The reason? There is no competition. Billboards don't exist anywhere in the state. Vermonters voted to ban them on all roads in the mid-1960's. It was the first—and last—anti-billboard law passed by a state in America. Vermonters will tell you that if other states had Vermont's scenic beauty, a number of such laws would have passed.

When ski season ends, March brings on maple season. During this time, it appears that every resident in the Kingdom has dropped other work and tapped into the business of syrup. If cold nights are followed by warm, windless days, sap runs well in the maples and farmers will boil it all night. "You've got to get right on it," says a worker at the Maple Grove Museum and Factory in St.

Johnsbury. "Some new syrup makers may come up here from Massachusetts and think they can wait a week to boil, but they can't. You've got to do it right away."

During peak season at the Maple Grove Factory, more than 90 employees bottle maple syrup and convert it into candy, maple cream and other products. Some of the employees are farm wives who have risen at 4:30 a.m., milked the cows, done the chores and then arrived at the factory to sort maple candies by hand.

While the factory churns out maple products in volume, small entrepreneurs are boiling like mad throughout the countryside. More signs appear by front doors and in yards. "Vermont maple syrup available here" is the message from almost every other household in the Kingdom. A number of makers add the words "Farm Prices" to their signs to assure you they're ready to deal.

Contrary to popular belief, sap does not rise in the maple tree; instead, it only flows out under pressure. The sap must then be piped to the sugar-house or else pulled there, either by tractor or by good old horse power. For the uninitiated visitor, any trip to maple country during peak season requires two indispensable aids: a good pair of boots, and the Vermont Agriculture Department's list of sugarhouses open to the public.

Summer in the fields of the Kingdom brings farm work: the growing of crops. At harvest time, some farms encourage visitors to pick their own strawberries, raspberries or vegetables. In the villages,

PICTURE-PERFECT MOORING
Newport City Dock, with its trim white window frames and flower boxes, serves as a safe anchorage for boaters on Lake Memphremagog—the long and narrow lake that extends north into Canada.

THE TRADING POST
The bulletin board at a Peacham store serves to keep everyone posted on community events and happenings. Vermonters in this part of the state are proud of their sense of community.

chicken pie supper at St. Michael's Church in Greensboro Bend. And community events don't end with Labor Day, either. Februarys in the past have found residents of Newport, in northern Orleans County, hosting Winterfest, an organized excuse to have as much fun in the cold as you can without doing something illegal.

What else could there be to do after watching an international dogsled race, fishing through the ice, ice-skating, cross-country skiing, taking a moonlight sleigh ride and staying up for a torchlight parade? The only remaining option might be to attend the Musher's Ball in honor of the dog race's valiant sled drivers.

TOWNS WITH NEIGHBORLY SPIRIT It isn't surprising that community events are so popular in the Northeast Kingdom. Community spirit ties the region together. If you look hard enough, you might find a village in the Kingdom that doesn't have a church with a white steeple, or one that doesn't have a general store with a gas pump. You might even find one that lacks an inn with multi-paned windows that give off a warm glow on cold winter nights. What you won't find is a village devoid of the bond that only good neighbors share.

It makes sense, after all. Most villages in the Northeast Kingdom are small. Yet, the nights are jet-black, the surroundings are rugged and help from the outside world isn't waiting around the next corner. In this remote region, people look to each other—not only for help in fighting isolation, but to share in enjoying the beauty of Northeast Vermont through the seasons.

Even the Kingdom's major center, St. Johnsbury, is really just a grownup village. Settled by Rhode Islanders in 1786, the town gained fame when Thaddeus and Erastus Fairbanks set up an iron foundry here, and began to turn out plows and measuring scales. The Fairbanks family planted their roots deep in the friendly soil of the Northeast Kingdom and over the years have given back much to the town where they made their name. In 1889, Franklin Fairbanks established the Fairbanks Museum and Planetarium in St. Johnsbury. Housed in an impressive red sandstone building, the museum's exhibits range from exotic birds to antique dolls.

Sit outside Willey's Store in Greensboro if you want to see community spirit. It's a weekday afternoon in mid-winter—very quiet, snow falling. Hardly a car or pedestrian passes in front of the pretty white houses on the village's tree-lined main street. Then a piercing wail shatters the snow-laden silence. It emanates from the firehouse just up the

festivals bloom. Vermonters have elevated the custom of organizing Ladies' Aid bazaars, firemen's picnics, banjo contests and other community events to an art form. Residents of the Northeast Kingdom contribute their fair share of such get-togethers to a statewide calendar that could keep a devotee of such events on the road nearly every weekend.

A sampling of summer events in the Kingdom might include: an antique gas and steam engine show at the Old Stone House Museum in Brownington; a lamplight service and hymn sing at the Old North Church in North Danville; and a

street. Ten seconds later, a pickup truck roars past; five seconds later, another. Both stop in front of the firehouse, where they are joined momentarily by several other vehicles. Men run from their trucks and their cars, disappearing into the firehouse. In what seems to be record time—less than five minutes after the fire alarm first sounded—fire trucks are speeding from the station and past Willey's Store. When there's a fire out there, it will be fought in short order by friends.

Even more neighborly spirit manifests itself inside Willey's. The store serves as a gathering place where villagers convene to complain about the weather, or to ask about how someone's relatives are doing. Willey's is built the same way a number of houses are constructed throughout the Northeast Kingdom. From the outside, it appears the two-story white clapboard structure has been added on to about 50 times. Additions jut out from the store's every corner. These, in turn, have spawned other additions, which take off in still-different directions. It would be downplaying the uniqueness of the store's jumbled roofline to characterize it as varied.

It is inside, however, that the store's freewheeling architectural spirit comes into its own. Walking its maze of narrow aisles, one senses the place must harbor a hardware section that by itself is half the size of Vermont. Squeaking your way across worn wooden floors, you will find an assemblage of merchandise that could keep a blockaded Greensboro thriving through the 21st century. Residents would not lack for cold cuts and videos; barn boots and wine; badminton shuttlecocks; Greensboro T-shirts emblazoned with giant beavers on dams; skunk scent for hunters (it masks human scent); suspenders, sledgehammers and putty.

In villages throughout the whole region, residents exhibit pride in the features that they feel make their part of the Kingdom unique. Derby Line, in northernmost Orleans County, boasts this unique trait: When you're strolling through town, half the time you're not sure just what country you're in at the moment. The border between Canada and the United States bisects the heart of this bilingual village. Neighborhood streets flow unhindered between the two countries. You certainly can't tell Vermont from Quebec just by the look of the houses.

Nowhere in the village is this blending of cultures more clearly exemplified than at the Haskell Free Library, an impressive stone and brick structure that features a library on the first floor and an opera house on the second. Not only does the border run through this building, it does so without slighting either Quebec or Vermont. In the library, you can find the right book in one country and check it out in the other. Upstairs, opera performers stand on stage in Canada, while their audience sits and applauds in the United States.

Fifty miles south, in the village of Cabot, residents also know what it feels like to live near a boundary line. Located about 15 miles west of St. Johnsbury, Cabot finds itself in Washington County, four miles from the Caledonia County line. Does this mean residents don't qualify as part of the Northeast Kingdom? Most books don't include their county when pinpointing the Kingdom's location.

But a difference of four miles does not change a person, the people of Cabot will tell you. They think they exemplify the toughness and spirit that set the Northeast Kingdom apart. Just look at their creamery, townspeople say. It took hard work and vision

AUTUMN TOUCHES
Residents of the Northest Kingdom delight in the change of seasons. With the approach of fall, home-grown creativity shows up on local porches and doors. Simple sprigs of Chinese lantern and red berries adorn a homemade wreath, left. And below, a bearded farmer and his wife greet passersby in Groton.

to establish it as a cooperative in 1919. Ninety-four farmers and 863 cows formed a union back then. Each founding family invested $5 per cow and a cord of wood. The Cabot Farmers' Creamery Cooperative still functions. It prospers, in fact, employing 200 people and collecting milk from 500 member farms.

Explaining the venture's success and longevity, a video presentation at the creamery's visitor center gives cows as much credit as people. The cooperative's bovine contributors are shown crossing back roads in a state of cleanliness practically unheard of in domestic livestock. Their art deco black and white splotches gleam spotlessly. A narrator lovingly describes them as "automated hydro-chemical conversion units" that produce 6 to 12 tons of milk per year.

Much of that milk goes toward cheddar cheese making. How good is the cheese? Imagine the cheer that went up in 1989, when residents learned that judges at the U.S. Championship Cheese Contest had voted the creamery's sharp cheddar the best cheddar cheese in the United States. What made the award all the sweeter was where it was given—

THE SOFT BRUSH OF WINTER
As winter settles its white cape over the hills, valleys and quiet towns of northeast Vermont, villages like Lower Waterford, at right, may look dormant. But Vermonters face the snow and cold with the same verve they show in summer and fall.

Green Bay, Wisconsin, right in the middle of established cheese country.

Few villages in the Northeast Kingdom can boast their own modern creamery. Few can match Derby Line's penchant for bilingual buildings. The truth is, however, it's people, not buildings, that matter.

Late on a January afternoon, in the tiny Orleans County village of Irasburg, children on ice skates hold hands as they whirl this way and that on a flooded section of the village common, which serves as the ice rink. Forty miles east, on the same frigid Sunday, other Northeast Kingdom residents—adults, teens and toddlers—are skating in the village of Island Pond. The Island Pond setting lacks the glamour of scenic New England. The rink is nothing more than a tiny park squeezed between a gas station and a car dealership. Yet the mood seems festive, despite the gloomy skies and a dank cold that cuts to the bone. Island Pond itself seems undaunted in the grip of winter. Its residents seem happy to be where they are—a little cold weather means nothing up here. How can it where people are blessed with that fierce independent spirit that thrives in the Kingdom?

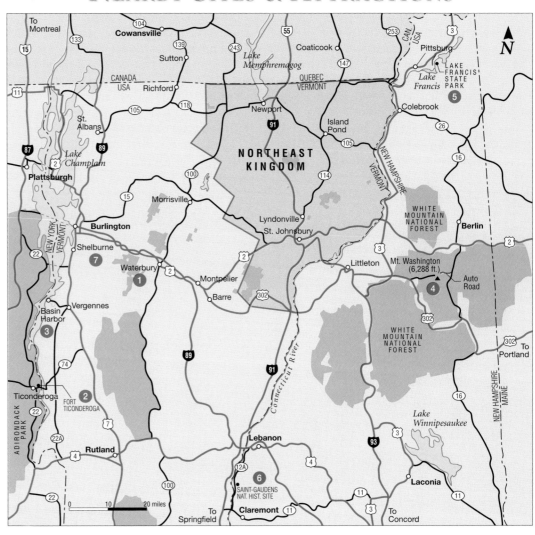

Mount Washington's cog railway, completed in 1869, was the first of its kind in the world. The little steam trains carry passengers up and down the mountain, a round trip of about three hours.

① BEN & JERRY'S ICE CREAM FACTORY, WATERBURY

Vermont's dairy industry has won the state numerous accolades. In 1977, Ben Cohen and Jerry Greenfield—two friends from Long Island, New York—came to the state to set up Ben & Jerry's ice cream company. Specializing in all-natural ingredients and rich flavorings, Ben & Jerry's has grown into a household name in the field of ice cream. The factory in Waterbury offers half-hour guided tours of the production area and research laboratory. Tours include a slide show on the history and philosophy of the company, a visit to Ben & Jerry's Hall of Fame and a free sample of the flavor of the day. Located in Waterbury off Hwy. 100.

② FORT TICONDEROGA

This stone fort, strategically located at the gateway to Lake Champlain, was built in 1755 by the French, who called it Fort Carillon. The star-shaped bastion was the scene of several fierce battles. In 1758, French troops repulsed an attack on the fort by a much larger British force. However, the British

gained possession of it in the following year. During the Revolution, Ticonderoga was captured by the Green Mountain Boys under the command of Ethan Allen and Colonel Benedict Arnold. Colonial forces withdrew in 1777, when the British hauled cannons to the summit of nearby Mt. Defiance, and the British then held the fort until the end of the war. The ruined fort was restored during the 19th century according to the original French plans, and today houses an impressive museum of weapons, paintings and uniforms. Located on Hwy. 74, 2 miles east of Hwy. 22.

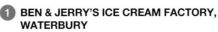

③ LAKE CHAMPLAIN MARITIME MUSEUM, BASIN HARBOR

Lake Champlain holds an honored place in American naval history. In 1776, Colonel Benedict Arnold led a motley fleet against the British at the Battle of Valcour Bay. Arnold's engagement delayed a British advance for a year. An exact replica of the 54-foot gunboat *Philadelphia*, one of the American ships lost in the engagement, forms the centerpiece of this museum, which interprets the colorful naval and maritime history of the lake and explains the science of nautical archeology. A restored schoolhouse contains a collection of artifacts, maps and model ships. There are also displays of boats built locally during the last 150 years, and a working forge where craftsmen demonstrate crafts both old and new. Located 6 miles west of Hwy. 7.

4 MOUNT WASHINGTON

New Hampshire's White Mountains are the highest in New England, and most of the range lies within the 750,000-acre White Mountain National Forest. At 6,288 feet in elevation, Mount Washington ranks as the highest peak in the White Mountains, as well as the highest in the northeastern United States. The weather on the mountain is frequently violent. A weather station on the summit has recorded winds of 231 miles per hour—the highest ever recorded. To reach the summit, visitors can take either the winding Mount Washington Auto Road (toll), or the historic cog railway. The railway departs from the Mount Washington Hotel at Bretton Woods, once billed as the largest wooden building in New England. At the summit of Mount Washington is a 54-acre state park, which boasts a post office, as well as a glassed-in observation building. Cog railway located off Hwy. 302; Auto Road located off Hwy. 16.

5 LAKE FRANCIS STATE PARK

The Connecticut River forms New Hampshire's western border with Vermont. Near its source lies Lake Francis State Park, located on an inlet of Lake Francis in the far north of the state. Lake Francis is the westernmost of a trio of lakes, the others being First and Second Connecticut. The park is a haven for wildlife: bald eagles, loons and woodpeckers are among the 123 bird species that have been sighted here. There are a number of hiking trails, including a three-mile trek up the slopes of Mount Galloway, the area's highest peak. Located east of Pittsburg off Hwy. 3.

6 SAINT-GAUDENS NATIONAL HISTORIC SITE

The country home, studio and gardens of the famed 19th-century sculptor Augustus Saint-Gaudens are preserved at this 150-acre site in the picturesque village of Cornish. The Dublin-born sculptor came to Cornish in 1885, and his presence attracted many other artists here. It was in Cornish that Saint-Gaudens executed most of his best-known works. These include the Shaw Memorial in Boston, statues of Admiral David Farragut and General William Sherman (both in New York), portraits of Abraham Lincoln, and the grave of Henry Adams's wife in Washington. Much of the artist's work is displayed here, along with gardens landscaped by Saint-Gaudens himself. The house, which was originally built around 1800 and once served as a tavern, includes rooms furnished in period style. On the site of the original sculpture studio (destroyed by fire in 1904) is a sculpture court, a gallery for special exhibitions and a studio for a sculptor-demonstrator. The site is located on Hwy. 12A.

7 SHELBURNE MUSEUM

This world-renowned museum is housed in a collection of some 37 buildings—including a covered bridge, a round barn and a Lake Champlain lighthouse. Many of the historic structures were moved from various locations in New England. Shelburne was founded in 1947 by Electra Havemeyer Webb and her husband J. Watson Webb to display their collection of folk art and Americana. Each building is filled with exhibits that include quilts, toys and dolls, game decoys, weathervanes, trade signs, maritime art, as well as European and American paintings and antiques. The Coach House displays the family's collection of carriages and sleighs. In the Shaker Shed, a range of household tools and implements reflects the simplicity and sobriety of the Shaker vision. One of the most fascinating exhibits is the paddle steamer *Ticonderoga*, which was moved overland from Lake Champlain in 1965. The museum is located on Hwy. 7 in the town of Shelburne.

An aerial view of the Shelburne Museum shows the 900-ton steamer Ticonderoga nestled incongruously amid the tranquil Vermont countryside. The ship carried passengers and cargo on Lake Champlain until the 1950's. The interior of the ship displays paintings, prints and photos depicting the steamboat era. In front of the ship stands the Colchester Reef Lighthouse, built in 1871 to warn ships away from one of Lake Champlain's most treacherous reefs. The lighthouse was moved to the museum grounds in 1952, and now houses a collection of ships' figureheads and scrimshaw (engraved sperm whale tooth). Among the many treasures displayed at the museum is the toy circus shown at left, made by a Pennsylvania Railroad brakeman for his children.

THE FINGER LAKES

Gouged from the land by relentless glaciers millions of years ago, they mark the heart of New York State.

The most beautiful images of the Finger Lakes region may be those captured by orbiting satellites. Racing overhead, satellite cameras capture what no earthbound observer can encompass: the symmetrical beauty of lakes clawed by nature into central New York's rolling hills. Viewed from above, side by side in a north-south alliance, these long, narrow lakes really do look like blue glacial fingers.

Some of the fingers are longer than others. Some cut deeper, some straighter. All trace their origin to the grinding of glacial advancement. Each one's bed was gouged out by ice sheets that pushed inexorably southward from Canada during the Ice Age.

The 11 lakes that resulted when these glacial gouges filled with water pay tribute to the force that created them. Seneca Lake, the region's deepest, boasts a maximum depth of more than 600 feet. Portions of its bottom are more than 200 feet below sea level. Cayuga, the longest Finger Lake, stretches 40 miles, is two miles wide at many

"Ithaca is gorges!" pronounce bumper stickers on cars around town. The play on words is an apt one. In what other metropolitan area, ask city boosters, can one reach several beautiful gorges within an easy walk of downtown? Ithaca's promoters neglect to mention that the walk, though short, is steep. Students who spend four years in this city leave it with lungs like mountain goats'. Up and down they go, drawn downtown from their hillside perches by Ithaca's eclectic blend of restaurants, book stores and shopping promenades.

TOWN AND COUNTRY

Near the center of town, in the former gymnasium of an old brick school building remodeled to house shops and offices, patrons ponder the intriguing bill of fare at the Moosewood Restaurant. Named for a species of maple tree that grows in the region and is browsed by moose in more northerly climes, the restaurant and its several cookbooks have gained regional prominence since Moosewood opened in 1973. A sunny Saturday finds patrons downing curried lentil soup, stuffed zucchini and other ethnic and vegetarian specialties.

Several blocks away, near the edge of the lake, the Ithaca Farmers' Market welcomes browsers to a large open-sided pavilion. Some shoppers come for the market's seasonal produce: cucumbers, lettuce, tomatoes, potatoes. Others peruse its ever-changing selection of pottery, hand-knit sweaters and other crafts. Vendors sell wheels of blue cheese and Mediterranean-style cheddar. Hot food aromas waft this way and that through the crowd.

While munching or shopping, visitors can gaze at the lake through the pavilion's open sides. With luck, the view will include members of the Cornell crew skimming across glassy waters in stiletto-shaped racing shells.

Ten miles up Cayuga's western shore, water moves with a much more purposeful force. At Taughannock Falls State Park, a sometimes-quick, sometimes-slow Taughannock Creek drops off the edge of a weathered rock cliff, then plunges 215 feet to a deep pool below. Higher than Niagara Falls, Taughannock is the highest straight-drop waterfall east of the Rocky Mountains.

If a summer thunderstorm strikes, drama quickly unfolds. The falls transforms from modest stream to cascading torrent in minutes. Observing it from viewing areas atop the gorge or below at its base, visitors watch as Taughannock Creek roars off the rim edge. Striking the pool below, its tumbling watery column erupts in a geyser-like explosion of mist and froth.

Downstream, where the creek empties into Cayuga Lake, early spring nights find strange ghost-

points and attains depths exceeding 400 feet. The other nine Finger Lakes boast less grandiose statistics, but are no less beautiful. Ranging from 3 to 16 miles long, they join their two larger neighbors in forming a region rich in the harmony of land interacting with water.

Occupying a roughly 9,000-square-mile area in the heart of central New York, the Finger Lakes lie within an easy day's drive from midtown Manhattan. Yet they are a world away in temperament. For the terrain surrounding these lakes is gentle and unhurried. This is a land of vineyard-covered slopes, which descend gradually to lakes some visitors liken to Norwegian fjords. It is a place of shady glens, summer-cool ravines and prosperous farms; a landscape where the lakes and their people join forces to create a mosaic of culture and natural beauty.

Nowhere is this union more perfectly showcased than in the City of Ithaca at Cayuga Lake's southern tip. Squeezed between the lake on one side and a series of steep hills on the other, this city of about 30,000 residents boasts scenic attractions as well as cultural flair.

Hilltop observers can gaze out beyond Ithaca toward Cayuga and the patchwork quilt pattern of farm fields and woodlots that descend to its cottage-lined shores. Both Ithaca College and Cornell University perch on hillsides that offer this classic Finger Lakes panorama. Cornell's beauty is enhanced by a spectacular gorge that cuts through its campus. Many Cornellians consider their college setting to be America's most scenic. Ithacans boast of their city in much the same way.

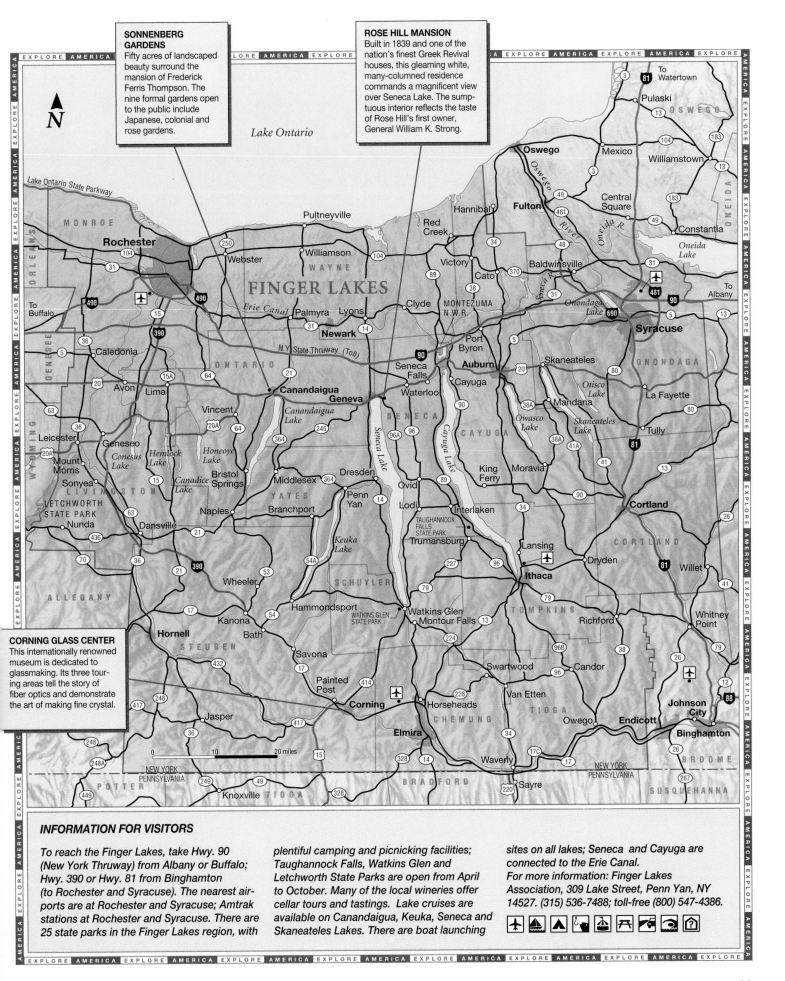

SONNENBERG GARDENS
Fifty acres of landscaped beauty surround the mansion of Frederick Ferris Thompson. The nine formal gardens open to the public include Japanese, colonial and rose gardens.

ROSE HILL MANSION
Built in 1839 and one of the nation's finest Greek Revival houses, this gleaming white, many-columned residence commands a magnificent view over Seneca Lake. The sumptuous interior reflects the taste of Rose Hill's first owner, General William K. Strong.

CORNING GLASS CENTER
This internationally renowned museum is dedicated to glassmaking. Its three touring areas tell the story of fiber optics and demonstrate the art of making fine crystal.

Lake Ontario

FINGER LAKES

N

INFORMATION FOR VISITORS

To reach the Finger Lakes, take Hwy. 90 (New York Thruway) from Albany or Buffalo; Hwy. 390 or Hwy. 81 from Binghamton (to Rochester and Syracuse). The nearest airports are at Rochester and Syracuse; Amtrak stations at Rochester and Syracuse. There are 25 state parks in the Finger Lakes region, with plentiful camping and picnicking facilities; Taughannock Falls, Watkins Glen and Letchworth State Parks are open from April to October. Many of the local wineries offer cellar tours and tastings. Lake cruises are available on Canandaigua, Keuka, Seneca and Skaneateles Lakes. There are boat launching sites on all lakes; Seneca and Cayuga are connected to the Erie Canal.
For more information: Finger Lakes Association, 309 Lake Street, Penn Yan, NY 14527. (315) 536-7488; toll-free (800) 547-4386.

CANYONS AND GORGES

Inspiration Point provides a dramatic look at the deep gorge and sheer cliffs of Letchworth State Park. Seventeen miles of the Genesee River Gorge is in the park, giving it its nickname as the Grand Canyon of the East.

VINES WITH A VIEW

The soil and moderate climate of the slopes of Seneca Lake produce ideal conditions for grapes. The region's wine industry goes back to 1829, when Reverend William Bostwick planted some grapes to make sacramental wine for his congregation. The area now produces hundreds of thousands of cases of wine each year. The grapes are also used for an area specialty, grape pie.

ly lights wavering over the water. Smelters are dipping. Armed with lanterns and long-handled wire mesh scoops, they have come to convert six-inch-long silvery fish called smelt into dinnertime fare. When instinct drives countless thousands of the smelt to migrate from the lake up small streams on nocturnal spawning runs, smelt fishermen stand at the ready.

Aided by lanterns, they plant themselves in the stream, squinting into the water for signs of a school darting by. At the merest sign of a flash their scoops dip into the water. If they're fast—and lucky—there'll be a dozen wriggling smelt in the scoop, glistening in the lantern's glow.

Enjoy them with Finger Lakes wine. You'll have plenty of varieties to choose from. The region boasts several dozen wineries. Vintners on lakes such as Cayuga, Seneca and Keuka have established "wine trails" for visitors. Simply follow the signs from one winery to the next. All the while you'll be driving through hillside vineyards that benefit from the lakes' tempering effect on a climate some might consider too harsh for producing good wine. That

TIES TO THE LAND
Shipshape red barns with smart white trim are evidence of the attention paid to the Finger Lakes' agricultural roots.

assumption would be false, because a growing number of New York State wines now compete with fine wines from all over the world. Many Finger Lakes wineries are small and family-operated. Chances are, if you stop for a tasting, the boss may be pouring the wine.

THE COMING OF THE VINIFERAS

At Vinifera Wine Cellars, north of Hammondsport on Keuka Lake, the boss is Willy Frank. The boss before him was his father, Konstantin Frank, who started the winery in the early 1960's. A native of Ukraine, Konstantin Frank came to America in 1951. He brought years of experience in the cultivation of Old World, or vinifera, grapes such as Riesling, Chardonnay and Pinot Noir. Konstantin Frank's challenge, he soon discovered, would be convincing Finger Lakes vintners that these grapes could be grown successfully in a climate famous for its icy winters.

Frank succeeded, however, and because of his efforts, a "vinifera revolution" began in the Finger Lakes region. It's still going on. Visitors traveling from vineyard to vineyard around Hammondsport and other Finger Lakes wine-making centers are hard pressed to find a winery that doesn't produce quality wines from vinifera grapes.

The roads between vineyards are well suited not only to wine tasting, but to wildlife observing. Sharp-eyed watchers will see white-tailed deer and wild turkeys—the turkeys sometimes eating the grapes. All the Finger Lakes attract waterfowl, especially during spring and fall migration. Early mornings witness wavering wedges of honking Canada geese flapping from the lakes, where they've slept, to adjacent cornfields, where they feed.

During recent years, the number of Canada geese wintering on the Finger Lakes has risen dramati-

HARVEST TIME

Pumpkins and gourds for sale at a roadside stand, above, are just part of the Finger Lakes' fall bounty, which includes green beans, New York apples, tomatoes and cabbages. Grapes are one of the region's prize crops; the lakes temper the seasonal variations in temperature, safeguarding the grapes from frost in spring and fall. Once the grapes have been harvested in late fall, morning frost and wisps of mist, right, start to blanket the land.

cally. Over Cayuga and Seneca Lakes, especially, tens of thousands of geese now fill the skies on December and January afternoons.

At the north end of Cayuga Lake, geese find an additional resting and feeding habitat at Montezuma National Wildlife Refuge, a vast freshwater wetland set aside by the federal government as a nature preserve in 1938. Wildlife watching is easy at Montezuma—so easy that visitors can watch birds without leaving their cars. A one-way "loop" road skirts Montezuma's main waterfowl pool. Vehicles creep along its three-and-a-half-mile length, their occupants scanning the pool's placid surface with binoculars and telescopes. For many observers Montezuma's birding rewards are substantial. One trip around the loop might yield a sighting of mallard ducks descending with cupped wings to land on the water with feather-light splashes. Another might turn up a basking turtle, a skulking heron or the serpentine tail of a swimming muskrat rippling the surface in S-shaped curves.

BRINGING BACK THE EAGLES

From 1976 until 1980, wildlife biologists used Montezuma as a release point for bald eagles brought from as far away as Alaska. The purpose of the release program was to reestablish America's national bird to New York State, where, by the 1960's, bald eagles had become practically extinct due to pesticide poisoning.

Removed from their nests shortly after hatching, the eaglets continued growing toward fledgling stage in artificial nests at Montezuma. Then they took to the wild on their own. In conjunction with subsequent eagle release sites throughout New York, the Montezuma release program has helped New York successfully bring back bald eagles. By the early 1990's, some 20 pairs of the majestic birds were nesting within state boundaries.

Travel any upstate New York highway, and you might spot an eagle soaring overhead. If you're on a bicycle, all the better. Because many Finger Lakes back roads are paved, yet lightly traveled, they provide excellent cycling conditions. Realizing this, companies in the region entice two-wheeled travelers to visit by offering bed-and-breakfast bicycle tours through the lakes country.

Inns and bed-and-breakfasts abound. The Sherwood Inn on Skaneateles Lake was built as a stagecoach stop and tavern in 1807. The doors of its unoccupied rooms are left open so guests can admire each room's wide-planked floors and authentic antique furnishings.

For Finger Lakes visitors enamored of walking, the prospects are no less appealing. Many hikers take advantage of the Finger Lakes Trail, an east-west footpath extending from the Catskill Mountains in eastern New York to Allegany State Park in the west. "One beautiful waterfall after another," is how many who travel the "FLT" describe it after walking its gorges and glens.

On its way through the Finger Lakes, the trail brushes the lower tip of Seneca Lake. Here, in the village of Watkins Glen, diversity banishes boredom. Strollers can climb through the world-famous gorge at Watkins Glen. Seekers of watery sights can partake of a dinner cruise up the lake. Lovers of speed and machines can converge on Watkins Glen International race track, a twisting, challenging

road course where the United States Grand Prix was held between 1961 and 1980. Engines still roar at "The Glen" every summer, thrilling thousands of fans, while Holstein cows in the nearby pastures don't seem impressed—or bothered—at all. Their attitude sums up the Finger Lakes mood: gentle, pastoral, relaxed.

Occasionally, of course, life buzzes with nervous excitement. An excellent example is the start of the annual bathtub race during Fillmore Days in the village of Moravia on Owasco Lake. Millard Fillmore, America's 13th president, was born just south of the village and, although he did not rev-

olutionize the office he assumed when Zachary Taylor died in 1850, he did—according to residents of Moravia—improve the plumbing in the White House. Thus, the commemorative bathtub race, in which tubs on wheels streak through the business district, pushed from behind by two contestants while a third steers from inside with a bathroom plunger.

In addition to Millard Fillmore, another notable, Jethro Wood, was born in Moravia. Wood made his name as the inventor of the cast-iron plow. But to date, no one has come up with an event to immortalize his contribution. All in good time.

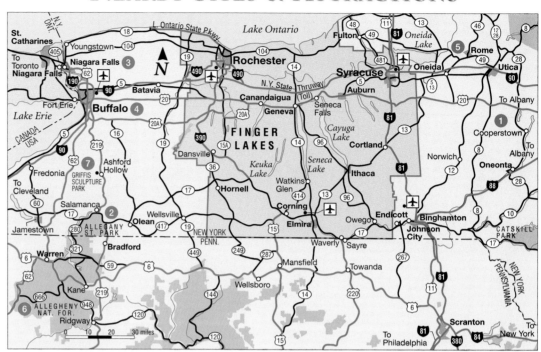

1 COOPERSTOWN

The National Baseball Hall of Fame and Museum in Cooperstown immortalizes more than 216 of baseball's greatest players. Life-size wood carvings of Babe Ruth and other baseball players are among the highlights of the museum along with artifacts, photographs and memorabilia tracing the history of the game. Included are a 19th-century catcher's mask, Old Judge baseball cards, and Babe Ruth's bat and ball. A multimedia presentation in the Grandstand Theater captures some of baseball's great moments. The Ballparks Room exhibits dugout benches, grandstand seats, and lockers from Forbes Field and Crosley Field. Cooperstown is also home to Fenimore House, an elegant mansion filled with extraordinary examples of American folk art. Several galleries in the house exhibit paintings, handpainted signs, weathervanes, hunting decoys, handmade quilts and sleighs. Located east of Syracuse on Hwy. 28.

2 ALLEGANY STATE PARK

Allegany State Park is the largest state park in New York. Eighty-five miles of hiking trails and many scenic drives zigzag through the park's 67,000 acres of rolling hills, thick, verdant forests and grassy meadowlands, dotted with lakes and streams. The park offers outdoor enthusiasts many year-round recreational activities, including hiking, bicycling, snowmobiling, tobogganing and cross-country skiing. Visitors are likely to spot some of the park's abundant wildlife, such as owls, white-tailed deer, wild turkeys, raccoons and black bears. Located south of Buffalo on Hwy. 17.

3 NIAGARA FALLS

Niagara Falls drops 185 feet at the rate of more than 200,000 cubic feet of water per second. The American Falls on the United States side and Horseshoe Falls on the Canadian side are separated by Goat Island. A bridge connects the island with the mainland. Elevators from Goat Island lead to Cave of the Winds where walkways take visitors behind American Falls, providing them with a dramatic view of the falls and upper rapids; rain gear is provided to protect visitors from the mist. Another exciting way to get a front-row-center look at the falls is to take a

The variety of architectural styles in downtown Buffalo reflects the city's long history as a prosperous commercial and manufacturing center, as well as its importance as a crossroads between east and west. The city is still an important transportation center, but is also home to a varied and active cultural life.

trip on the *Maid of the Mist*, an excursion boat that goes directly in front of the Falls. Located off Hwy. 190 on the Robert Moses Parkway.

4 BUFFALO

The opening of the Erie Canal in 1825 made Buffalo one of the main transportation centers in the nation. The St. Lawrence Seaway, inaugurated in 1959, ensured the city's prosperity; today, it is the second largest city in the state. The Theodore Roosevelt Inaugural National Historic Site on Delaware Avenue was the location of the inauguration of Roosevelt in 1901 as the 26th president of the United States, hours after the death of the assassinated President William McKinley. This stately mansion, built in the Greek style, and furnished with period pieces, is open to the public. The Albright-Knox Art Gallery's world-class collection includes sculpture from 3000 B.C. to the present, but is best known for contemporary painting and sculpture by such artists as Picasso, Renoir, Andy Warhol and Jackson Pollock. The observation tower at City Hall provides a panoramic view of Lake Erie and the province of Ontario, Canada. Located on Hwy. 90 (New York State Thruway).

5 ROME

The city of Rome is located along a portage road, called Oneida Carry, the overland section of an ancient water route that linked the Great Lakes with the Atlantic Ocean. The British built Fort Stanwix here in 1758 to protect the portage during the French and Indian War. During the Revolution, the fort was used by American troops to defend the Mohawk Valley. In 1777, a garrison of 550 American soldiers inside the fort withstood a siege by British and Indian forces. The earth-and-log fort has been reconstructed and costumed interpreters reenact military life during the Revolutionary War. Visitors can also take a trip on an 1840's mule-drawn canal packet boat along a restored section of the Erie Canal to the Erie Canal

Village. The village's original buildings include a tavern, church, blacksmith shop, millinery shop, train station, schoolhouse, manor home and settlers' cabins. The Canal Museum exhibits paintings, models and photographs that tell the history of the canal. Located on Hwy. 49.

6 ALLEGHENY NATIONAL FOREST

The 510,536 acres of the Allegheny National Forest contain several unique natural environments. One of them, a 100-acre area called Heart's Content, contains virgin stands of hemlock, white pine, sugar maple, beech and black cherry trees. A 1¼-mile interpretative trail meanders through the thick forest; at the end of the trail is an exhibit on the early days of logging in the region. Reservoirs located 20 miles from Heart's Content are stocked with trout, walleye, northern pike and bass. The Buzzard Swamp Wildlife Area is one of the best places to spot wildlife in the forest—especially migratory waterfowl. Birdwatchers can also spot hawks, osprey, woodpeckers and Pennsylvania songbirds along the Songbird Sojourn hiking trail. Located on Hwys. 6 and 62.

7 GRIFFIS SCULPTURE PARK

Walking trails crisscross this 400-acre park of meadowland, ponds and gently rising hills. More than 200 sculptures of welded steel, wood, aluminum, ceramic and bronze are displayed in this natural setting, the work of several artists. The sculptures range from representational to abstract, and are divided into 12 groups with evocative names such as The Fecund Figures, The East Hill Birds, The King, Queen and Bishop, The Tower, Submarine and Bathysphere and The Insect Series. The Ashford Hollow Foundation for the Visual and Performing Arts has maintained the sculpture park since 1969. The park is open from May through October. Located on Ahrens Road, off Hwy. 219.

Niagara Falls' tumbling cascades, one of the world's most famous natural wonders, have delighted visitors for decades. The falls span the border between the United States and Canada.

THE CHESAPEAKE

Chesapeake Bay's magical light brings water and clouds together in a seamless horizon.

Even the ground seems in league with the sea. Creeks, channels, rivers and swamps wander inland among broad fertile fields and sudden forests, lapping at the weathered docks of villages little changed since the nation began. Look in the distance almost anywhere and you may see the linear flash of Chesapeake Bay water, the delicate leaning arc of a wind-filled sail. Or, in still another direction, a mighty roll of Atlantic Ocean. This fusion of sea and land is at the heart of everything in Chesapeake country, especially on the Eastern Shore of Maryland and Virginia.

Against all odds, "the Shore"—as the 150-mile-long peninsula is styled in the regional lexicon—has retained its ancient character, an authentic difference, despite a proximity to the Middle-Atlantic region's population goliaths. From the heart of the Maryland Shore, it's a drive of only 90 minutes to either Washington or Baltimore, and two hours to Philadelphia. On the Virginia end, Norfolk and Virginia Beach lie within half an hour's drive.

BAY TREASURES

An abandoned flat-bottomed boat lies grounded amid the dune grasses on Assateague Island. The barrier island stretches 50 miles in a north-south direction and embraces Chincoteague Bay, whose waters are generally shallow and a good place for clamming and crabbing. Just beyond the shadow of the gigantic red-and-white Assateague Lighthouse, the beach at Assateague Island National Seashore is one of the nation's best, unsurpassed as an East Coast destination for public surfing and swimming.

SOLO SAILING

Overleaf: A solitary sailboat makes barely a ripple in the still waters of the Shore's watery realm. Seen from the air, Chesapeake Bay reveals its offshoot rivers and inland channels, which snake their way through the fields and forests of the peninsula.

And what gateways beckon travelers from busy megalopolis to the Shore's watery realm! From mainland Annapolis, just east of Washington, D.C., the Chesapeake Bay Bridge links the mainland with the peninsula. From Virginia Beach, far to the south, the 17.6-mile-long Chesapeake Bay Bridge-Tunnel alternately skims above the whitecaps and plunges into briny depths, crossing the very mouth of Chesapeake Bay where the Atlantic begins, between mainland Virginia Beach and the Shore's Cape Charles.

TOWN AND COUNTRY HERITAGE	Maryland's Shore is larger than Virginia's, and neatly divides into northern and southern halves of four counties each. A

visitor notes scant difference in the landscape, although the northern Shore tends to be a bit more undulating than the southern. To apply the adjective "hilly" anywhere in this sea-girt land is generally a stretch. Mostly, it's flat. But whatever the county, the Shore's heritage lives indelibly in its farmland and venerable towns. Together, they comprise some of the nation's most delightful places to live, work and visit.

Consider Chestertown, Maryland, founded 1706, seat of Kent County and the Shore's northern outpost. Baltimore lies only 25 miles west across the Bay, but it seems light years from this colonial port on the Chester River about 12 miles inland. Chestertown even had its own version of the Boston Tea Party. In May 1774, angry residents boarded a brigantine docked near the Custom House and tossed overboard its cargo of high-tax tea. The Custom House is still there on Water Street, one of the sights of a walking tour of old Chestertown. There's a sense of timeless Americana, the look of

PEERLESS PIER

Fishermen cast their lines for bluefish, trout, flounder—and even shark— from the 625-foot-long Sea Gull Fishing Pier. The pier is located on the first of four man-made islands that form part of the Chesapeake Bay Bridge-Tunnel. An engineering marvel, the bridge is the largest bridge-tunnel complex in the world.

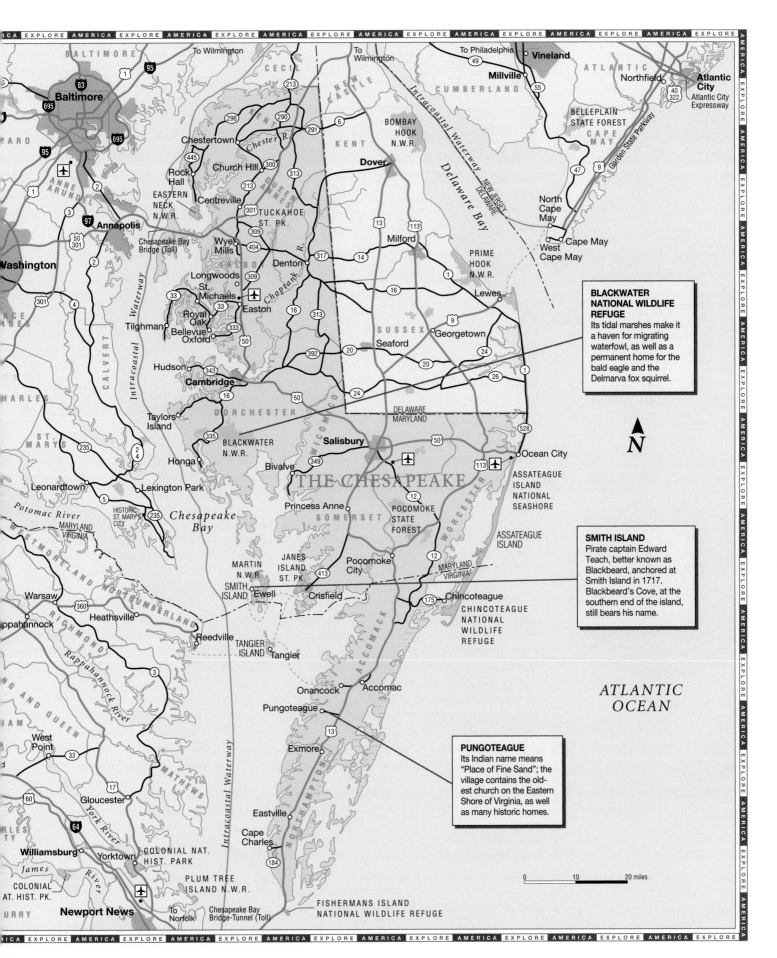

BLACKWATER NATIONAL WILDLIFE REFUGE
Its tidal marshes make it a haven for migrating waterfowl, as well as a permanent home for the bald eagle and the Delmarva fox squirrel.

SMITH ISLAND
Pirate captain Edward Teach, better known as Blackbeard, anchored at Smith Island in 1717. Blackbeard's Cove, at the southern end of the island, still bears his name.

PUNGOTEAGUE
Its Indian name means "Place of Fine Sand"; the village contains the oldest church on the Eastern Shore of Virginia, as well as many historic homes.

The majestic twin suspension spans of the Chesapeake Bay Bridge, formally known as the William Preston Lane Memorial Bridge, curve up and over in a graceful sweep, above ship channels, islands and beaches. The bridge serves as the main gateway to Maryland's Eastern Shore.

A basket of freshly harvested blue crabs attest to the rich waters of Chesapeake Bay. Blue crabs are one of the region's seafood delicacies. In traditional crab houses, the crabs are steamed, then cracked with mallets.

centuries spent blending. Chestertown is where the movie theater still plays on brick-sidewalked High Street, and where, after the matinee, it's nice to drop into nearby Stam's Drug Store, another vintage gathering place, for one of their celebrated ice cream sodas. A visitor comes away thinking that Norman Rockwell would have loved Chestertown.

DRAMATIC RURAL BACKDROP

The landscape of Queen Annes County, south of Kent, is dominated by the same careful agriculture that imposes a manicured look across much of the Shore. Wide, deep fields of corn and wheat lead the eye to horizons crowned by massive white farmhouses. These steep-roofed, gabled, angular structures, juxtaposed on well-groomed fields, help create an almost theatrical rural panorama.

Highway 213, its cheerful scenic route signs depicting Maryland's state flower (the black-eyed Susan), wends its way through such vistas from Chestertown south to Centreville, the seat of Queen Annes County. Smaller than Chestertown, Centreville owns much of the same antique allure. Its white courthouse, dating from 1791, is Maryland's oldest in continuous use. Boxwood-lined brick pathways lead under elms and lindens in the tranquil setting of Courthouse Square, shielded by a statue of Queen Anne. Narrow streets, framed with the architectural amalgam of three centuries, are one-way by modern necessity. One carries northbound traffic; another southbound,

and between them the town unfolds in a tidy visual package embracing the courthouse as well as charm-rich 18th-century residences.

Highway 213 meanders southward from Centreville across two busy thoroughfares, US 301 and US 50, before changing its designation to Highway 662 in Talbot County near the historic village of Wye Mills. Tree fanciers may want to pause for a look at the leafy span of Wye Oak, Maryland's official tree, claimed to be the largest white oak in America and more than 450 years old. Nearby is a working gristmill of equally astounding age: Wye Mill ground its first corn in 1671, and was already a century old when it made flour for Washington's Continentals in the Valley Forge winter of 1778.

But Talbot County is better known for a quartet of other historic communities. Less than 75 miles east of Washington, D.C., the towns of Easton, Oxford, St. Michaels and Tilghman cluster like the points of a parallelogram, each about 10 miles from the next. Easton, the largest, is a cosmopolitan little city with roots deep in the 17th century. Much of the downtown architecture seems Victorian at first viewing, but look carefully—the streets reveal much greater age. The Third Haven Friends Meeting House of 1682 may be America's oldest frame house of worship in continuous use. The Georgian courthouse of Talbot County has dominated the heart of town since 1794. Such gems of downtown Easton are best appreciated by taking a self-guided walking tour, as laid out by the

Historical Society of Talbot County. Its headquarters (in a tall Federal mansion of 1810) is a good place to begin. The society also operates a museum with rotating exhibitions.

Easton's cultural depth is surprising for such a small town. The Academy of Arts stages a series of exhibitions and performances, and there is the Celebration of the Arts each spring. This being the Shore, where the sky is rarely void of waterbirds, the year's biggest event is the Waterfowl Festival.

From landlocked Easton, scenic Highway 333 leads in a matter of minutes to Oxford, oldest port town on the Maryland Shore. Settled in the 1660's, it became one of Maryland's two official ports of entry in 1694. For almost a century it thrived, but after the Revolution Oxford entered a long, lazy cycle of alternating slumber and revival. Yet it retained a proud seafaring tradition in every age, and the foursquare middle-class homes of working watermen took their places beside the mansions of vanished colonial nabobs.

In our time, Oxford's period allure is polished by prosperity and tasteful restorations. Morris Street, the principal avenue, runs wide and straight along the point of land between the Tred Avon River and Town Creek, a distance of some five blocks. The homes and venerable stores of Morris Street mix gracefully without a discordant note. Many wear sophisticated color schemes. And while gift shops and boutiques have taken over the plain sturdy stores that once supplied hard-handed crabbers and oystermen, they have treated the old buildings with care and respect, preserving such original features as interior counters and shelves. A small museum at the corner of Morris and Market dis-

SHAGGY AND STURDY
Two herds of wild ponies live on Assateague Island, left; the herds are separated by a fence at the boundary between Maryland and Virginia. In Virginia, the ponies are permitted to graze on the Chincoteague National Wildlife Refuge. Below, parallel fences protect the drifting sand dunes on Chincoteague Island. Famous for its oysters and clams, the island is popular with beachcombers and beach lovers alike.

RIVER VIEW

RIVER VIEW
The majestic mansions of Water Street in Chestertown line the Chester River just as they have since before the American Revolution. The town was a port of entry in colonial times and thrived during the 18th century, when many of these elegant homes were built by affluent shippers and merchants.

plays memorabilia from the town that was, with emphasis on its history as a boatbuilding center.

OXFORD ON THE TRED AVON

One of America's finest historic inns (and purveyor of perhaps the world's best crab cakes) overlooks the Tred Avon waterfront in a structure built by ship's carpenters before 1710. The Robert Morris Inn was the home of the father of Robert Morris, Jr., financier of the American Revolution. Nearby, the Oxford Custom House, a reproduction of the original 1690's structure nattily painted in shades of pale tan, rust and camel, stands behind its white picket fence. The Oxford waterfront seems placid, immaculate, conservatively upscale, with waterfront homes of tidy rectitude and long private piers in perfect trim.

These days, the harbor stirs mostly with the arrival and departure of the Oxford-Bellevue Ferry, a service that began in 1683. A half-dozen or so waiting cars roll onto the white, green-trimmed little diesel-powered *Talbot* for the voyage of about 10 minutes across the mile-wide Tred Avon. On the Bellevue shore the waterfront is one of plain docks and fishing boats, the habitat of working watermen. Bellevue Road then traverses a rural scene through fields spangled with wild geese, passing the village of Royal Oak, and soon intersecting with Highway 33, the road to St. Michaels and Tilghman Island.

For many visitors, St. Michaels is the star civic attraction of the Eastern Shore. And for good reason. Here are gathered choice examples of the history—and the icons—that make the area what it is. From origins in the 1670's, St. Michaels went on to become an important shipbuilding port. In the War of 1812, facing a night attack by British warships, townspeople blacked out the lights of their buildings and, hoisting lanterns into the trees, caused the British to miss their targets.

Boatbuilding and shellfishing occupied St. Michaels for another century and a half or so, but recent years brought the town a new focus: the Chesapeake Bay Maritime Museum. On 18 acres of harborfront, the museum touches the very heart of Bay history and culture. Moored at the docks are classic specimens of boats once made here. The *Edna Lockwood*, a two-masted bugeye delectable in white and butterscotch paint, was built at nearby Tilghman Island in 1889 and, on retirement in 1967, was the last bugeye to dredge for oysters. Another classic sail-powered workboat docked at the museum, the skipjack *Rosie Parks*, was also famously fast, winning more skipjack races than any other. More about such legends emerges in the Bay of Chesapeake Building. Here is the complete perspective on the Bay's history and culture, including Indians and their log canoes, an 18th-century dock and factor's office, and a gallery showing the best of today's maritime artists. The artistry of decoys, and the Bay's role in the Atlantic flyway, are emphasized in the Waterfowling Building. The museum's biggest artifact is the six-sided Hooper Strait Lighthouse, a white structure like a cottage on pilings surmounted by a giant cupola. Visitors scramble up steep stairs to marvel at the great light's shining, complex Fresnel lens.

Clusters of black-eyed Susans, the state flower of Maryland, brighten the back roads of the region. The state's scenic route signs proudly display this symbol.

A statue of Queen Anne stands on the courthouse green in Centreville, a visual reminder that the town was chartered as the seat of Queen Annes County in 1794. The courthouse has been in continuous use since 1791, making it the oldest house of justice in Maryland.

Those inspired by such nautical goings-on need only walk a few feet across the docks to find a cruise of their liking. Some have a historic emphasis; others, guided by marine biologists, concentrate on natural history. Non-sailors may take a self-guided walking tour of the streets of St. Michaels. Blocks of ancient buildings still crowd the narrow passageways, but the ambience tilts decidedly to the tourist trade. Homes of vanished sea captains have become bed-and-breakfast inns and boutiques; an old general store now purveys upscale sportswear. The character of it all is good, even polished, and a banner-bedecked sense of gaiety prevails.

Some 12 miles farther along Highway 33, at Tilghman, a visitor strikes the Bay's authentic essence, a scene worthy of the phrase, "picturesque fishing village." Framed by Knapps Narrows and the hyperactive drawbridge across it, this hard-working little watermen's town seems a jumble of white hulls, packing sheds, refrigerated seafood trucks and austere white houses in perfect trim. The alert traveler should look especially sharply at the Tilghman harbor, for this is the chief home port for a tiny handful of working skipjacks. As of 1993, only 20 of the legendary sailboats still went oystering, and of those, 14 claimed Tilghman as

their home port. But if the oyster business was in decline, crabbing and fishing endured. For visiting sport fishermen, Tilghman Island is a noted center for accommodations and charters. Allowing for seasonal changes, the game fish quarry includes bluefish, trout, striped bass, croakers and perch.

	Returning to US 50 and point-
WINGED	ing south, travelers soon cross
VISITORS	the Choptank River to Cam-
FLOCK IN	bridge, and enter the Southern
	Eastern Shore. Cambridge

enjoys one of the most scenic locations on the peninsula, with its ancient town center gathered on low hills beside a sheltered harbor. Brick-paved High Street displays a notable collection of mansions, some more than 200 years old. For many visitors, though, the greatest attraction in the Cambridge orbit is the Blackwater National Wildlife Refuge, 20,090 acres of mostly tidal marsh that teems with birds and mammals. A drive through may introduce Canada and snow geese, tundra swans, more than 20 species of ducks, bald eagles, peregrine falcons, muskrats, red fox, otters and the endangered Delmarva fox squirrel. The peak period is from mid-October to mid-March.

But it's always peak period for birds at Salisbury, about 30 miles southeast. Forget that the Shore's largest town calls itself the poultry capital of the world. The birds that people come to see are exquis-

ite carvings, antique decoys and paintings in the new 30,000-square-foot Ward Museum of Wildfowl Art. Opened in 1992, the handsome structure beside a Salisbury pond is infinitely more than a decoy museum. The brothers for whom it was named, the late Lem and Steve Ward of Crisfield, carved their way from traditional working decoys into a new decorative bird art form. Wildfowl art, jewel-like in its realism, has become hugely popular, and the Ward Museum's nine galleries exhibit permanent collections and changing exhibitions.

The counties around Salisbury—Wicomico, Somerset and Worcester—collectively span the entire Southern Maryland Shore from Bay to Atlantic. Bayside interest often focuses on Crisfield, where the National Hard Crab Derby and Fair occurs each Labor Day weekend, and where cruise boats and ferries depart for Smith Island, Maryland, and Tangier Island, Virginia, two tiny populated keys in the middle of the bay where descendants of early British settlers still harvest their livelihood from the sea. Another traditional touch occurs each Labor Day off Deal Island (accessible by car), when the Bay's skipjacks gather to race. Less salty activities prevail in the town of Princess Anne, whose historic district stages tours of colonial homes on the second weekend in October.

Yet the great dynamo of the region is on the Atlantic side, where Ocean City unfurls its 10-mile strand of boardwalk, hotels, nightclubs, restaurants and charter boat docks. The Virginia border—resting on the 38th parallel—introduces a part of the peninsula that shares many of Maryland's traits, yet retains a stout identity of its own. The Atlantic is more a factor here than in Maryland. Although the Virginia Shore is smaller than Maryland's, its oceanfront is more than twice as long. Roughly 70 miles long and only 5 to 10 miles wide, the Virginia peninsula is served by one main thoroughfare: Highway 13. Visitors can be whisked along convenient, fast and misleading "13" through two entire counties, convinced that Virginia's Shore is a hodgepodge of flat fields, gigantic chicken sheds and commercial roadside clutter. In truth, an exploration down almost any side road can lead to drowsing scenes of farms and forests, obscure watermen's villages, the white surprise of cotton fields, and ancient courthouse towns where clocks and calendars move fitfully. There is a saying on the Virginia Shore: We're 50 miles from Norfolk, and 50 years.

Look at Accomac, seat of Accomack County since about 1660, yet even now counting a population less than 500. In the clerk's office visitors can see books dating to 1663, the nation's second-oldest set of continuous court records, including one where an early patriot inscribed the words: "God Damn the King." Accomac reminds some visitors of a small unrestored Williamsburg, doubtless because of its number of 18th-century buildings, some of them grand brick mansions with numerous endwise add-ons in the distinctive Virginia Shore style known as "big house, little house, colonnade and kitchen." Yet the most interest seems generated by a small brick structure in the jailyard: the county's debtor's prison of 1783.

It is a measure of the Virginia Shore's place in time that the oldest set of continuous court records in the United States is only 30-odd miles south. That honor—unbroken chronicles since 1632—goes to Eastville, seat of Northampton County. The scene around Eastville's Courthouse Green is a time capsule of Virginia history. Although the present courthouse (the county's sixth) dates only from 1899, the town has preserved the version of 1731, from which the Declaration of Independence was read in 1776. Nearby is a brick debtor's prison of uncertain but extreme age, a row of little frame lawyers' offices, and the Eastville Inn of about 1760. Monuments honor local Confederate soldiers and

"The Laughing King," an Indian leader who befriended the first English settlers.

If there were community laurels for antiquity, setting and contemporary comfort—in other words, all-around appeal—they might go to the bayside port of Onancock. There is no telling the settlement's age; Indians had the site first, calling it "Foggy Place"; white settlers visited in 1621. Onancock became an official Virginia port in 1680. More than 300 years later, the port still functions with some commercial shipping. It is also home harbor for a passenger ferry to Tangier Island, a cruise which takes about 90 minutes each way. Onancock's architecture mixes the many periods of its long history. Its most distinguished ornament is probably the Kerr (pronounced *kar*) Place, a brick mansion of 1799, now the home of the Eastern Shore of Virginia Historical Society. With period rooms and museum displays, Kerr Place is a rare thing on the Shore: a historic home regularly open to the public.

Such tranquil pleasures are often overlooked by the throngs of people heading for the Virginia Shore's undisputed touristic champions, Chincoteague and Assateague. That pair of linked oceanside islands—combining a spectacular beach, a major national wildlife refuge as well as the fishing port of Chincoteague—is a beguiling destination indeed, though sometimes it seems that tourists outnumber not only the famous herd of wild ponies that roam the islands, but the vast waterbird population too.

A quieter alternative for greeting the Atlantic Ocean lies through The Nature Conservancy, an international conservation group that owns all or part of 14 barrier islands south of Assateague. These islands comprise an astounding 40-plus miles of Virginia coastline. The gateway to this 35,000-acre realm of islands and beaches is the Conservancy's Virginia Coast Reserve, which is headquartered at Nassawadox in Northampton County. By advance reservation only, naturalists lead boat excursions through game-rich salt marshes and channels to oceanfront beaches as unspoiled as the day the first settlers arrived.

From such shell-strewn beaches, where the surf booms and mutters unrestrained by jetty, pier or condominium, Norfolk seems much farther away than 50 miles. Or even 50 years.

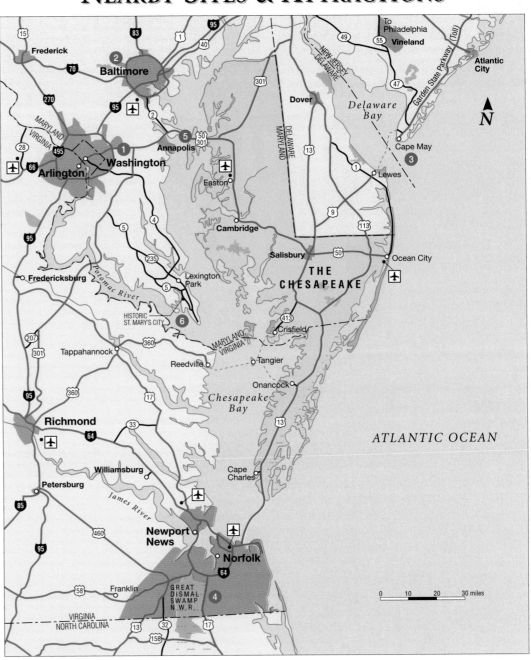

NEARBY SITES & ATTRACTIONS

The Maryland Dove *is an authentic, working reconstruction of the supply ship that accompanied English colonists on their three-month voyage to the New World. The colonists founded a settlement on the Potomac River, which they called St. Mary's City. The original ship crossed the Atlantic only once. Worms attacked the ship's timbers, and the vessel sank on its way back to England in 1634. The 42-ton replica was commissioned in 1978.*

Cape May's picturesque wooden houses were mainly built during the 1800's, when the New Jersey seaside town enjoyed wide popularity as a summer resort. Many of the houses are brightly painted or sport elaborate wrought ironwork and gingerbread.

❶ WASHINGTON

Washington's broad, tree-lined avenues and noble public spaces complement landmarks such as the White House, the Capitol Building, the Washington Monument and the Lincoln Memorial. The city brims with museums and galleries, including the National Gallery of Art, the Phillips Collection and the renowned Smithsonian Institution. Washington is located on Hwys. 95 and 270.

❷ BALTIMORE'S INNER HARBOR

The revitalized Inner Harbor is a lively area of shops, restaurants, museums, art galleries, churches and historic sites. Two of the most popular attractions are the Maryland Science Center, with its displays of energy, optics and magnetism, and the National Aquarium, which houses more than 5,000 species of animals and plants. A number of historic ships are permanently moored in the Inner Harbor. Located northeast of Washington on Hwys. 95 and 40.

❸ CAPE MAY

In the early 1800's, the little whaling port of Cape May became a fashionable seaside resort for wealthy New Yorkers and Philadelphians. A collection of some 600 ornate Victorian wooden houses make up the town's Historic District, which has been declared a National Historic Landmark. Cape May's architectural bounty has been extensively restored since the 1960's. Visitors can take a walking tour of the historic district, or explore the area aboard a vintage trolley bus or open carriage. Located at the southern end of the Garden State Parkway.

4 GREAT DISMAL SWAMP NATIONAL WILDLIFE REFUGE

In days of sail, mariners prized the tannin-stained waters from Great Dismal Swamp, which were said to stay fresh indefinitely. Significant stands of cypress, juniper and pine trees grow on islands amid the bogs, creeks and pools of the swamp, and the juices and resins of the trees help to purify the water. Hundreds of bird species inhabit this 107,000-acre refuge, which is also home to black bears, bobcats, otters, white-tailed deer and several species of snakes. Lake Drummond, an 18-mile-square stretch of open water in the heart of the swamp, offers good fishing. Located south of Suffolk off Hwy. 32.

5 ANNAPOLIS

The capital of Maryland boasts the greatest concentration of 18th-century buildings in the nation. In the 1700's, it was Maryland's main port, and its wealthy merchants built impressive brick mansions. Visitors can take walking tours of the Colonial Annapolis Historic District. The United States Naval Academy was founded here in 1845, and the 300-acre campus is home to 4,200 midshipmen. The Academy Museum surveys more than 300 years of American naval history, and includes paintings, weapons and naval memorabilia. The Gallery of Ships houses a fine collection of more than 100 warship models, some dating back to the 17th century. The monumental chapel features Tiffany stained glass windows depicting naval heroes, as well as the tomb of John

Paul Jones, whose remains were brought from Paris in 1905. Located northeast of Washington on Hwys. 50 and 301.

6 HISTORIC ST. MARY'S CITY

In 1634, two small ships brought a group of English colonists to the eastern shore of the Potomac River. After purchasing an Indian village, they built their own settlement on the site. Named for the Virgin Mary, St. Mary's City served as the capital of Maryland until 1695. No original structures survive, but the site is the focus of archeological research. Several buildings have been reconstructed, including the old State House. On the Godiah Spray Tobacco Plantation, costumed interpreters recreate the life of a plantation family during the 1600's. Located 6 miles south of Lexington Park, off Hwy. 5.

The leafy Historic District occupies the middle ground in this aerial view of Annapolis. Colonial Annapolis owed its prosperity to its port, and the town has maintained strong links with the sea. The massive bulk of the United States Naval Academy, established at Annapolis in 1845, lies adjacent to the district along the Severn River.

Stately Doric columns guard the entrance to the Lincoln Memorial in Washington, D.C. The 19-foot-high statue of the assassinated president was fashioned from 20 blocks of Georgia marble.

POTOMAC HIGHLANDS

*Here is the heart of the Alleghenies, a land
where rivers rise—a region of mountains,
forests, streams and open valleys.*

Approaching the Highlands from the east, from the broad and luminous Shenandoah Valley, two-lane roads curl upward into mysterious ramparts darkened by screens of ancient hemlocks, through narrow sheer canyons streaked with clear rushing streams, past small traditional farms of red barns, white houses and black cattle. On some lofty summit a marker proclaims the state line, and soon a mountaineer will be waving cheerily from the roadside. Welcome, he means to say, to the Allegheny Front, the Potomac Highlands, the State of West Virginia.

There is good reason to apply the name Potomac Highlands to this part of eastern West Virginia. The great river's headwaters do rise here: North Branch, South Branch, North Fork South Branch, South Fork South Branch. And there are other local streams with names such as Lost River and Cacapon River and Patterson Creek, whose crystal waters eventually will join the Potomac coalition, pick up the Shenandoah at Harpers Ferry and flow (a bit roiled by the journey) into the nation's capital some 200 miles away. Soon all this confluence flows into Chesapeake Bay and then into the Atlantic. So labyrinthine, so geologically tumultuous is the region that, side by side with the eastbound Potomac tributaries, other rivers also rise—and stubbornly set forth in other directions.

Not surprisingly, the form, the character, even the precise dimensions of such a place as the Potomac Highlands resist easy description. But picture a ragged-edged rectangle measuring about 180 by 45 miles, slanting southwest to northeast, and bordering both Maryland and Virginia. Apart from the abiding mountains and lovely streams, the region is unified by the massive presence of Monongahela National Forest. Across nine counties, this 901,000-acre treasury of public land is never far from towns, farms and roadsides.

The land, much of it wilderness today, was reclaimed by the United States Forest

An early morning autumn fog swirls around white-water rafters as they tackle the Gauley River. The Highlands contain 24 headwater streams that feed some of the best white-water streams in the U.S.

Overleaf: The jutting rocky cliffs of Tuscarora sandstone attract serious rock climbers to Seneca Rocks. A less arduous trail leads hikers to the summit, where they are rewarded with an impressive view of the ancient green mountains.

Service around the time of World War I from heavily cut, barren timberland. Over some 70 years, reforestation has been joined by an increasing commitment to the development of recreational facilities so that the public now enjoys some 700 miles of marked trails and 20 campgrounds. The forest is a bonanza for hikers, climbers, picnickers, canoers and rafters, cross-country skiers, campers, birdwatchers, fishermen and hunters.

One trademark vista seems to dramatize the very essence of the region as both a striking landscape and a challenge to humankind's daring and endurance—a symbol that the Highlands' ultimate challenges are not for the faint of heart. A traveler driving east from Elkins on Highway 33, after passing through some spectacular scenery near the village of Onego, looks up to an astonishing apparition: a gray, ragged, alpinelike cliff rising about 1,000 feet above a green meadow at the floor of North Fork Valley in Pendleton County. It is like a somber frill, an ornament from another geologic time, jutting forth from the huge Allegheny Mountain behind it. This is Seneca Rocks, certainly one of the more theatrical natural curiosities in a state that is filled with them.

For about a century now, Seneca Rocks has been a shrine for rock climbers. Often they can be seen dangling, like slow-moving spiders, from the grooved, cracked, eroded front wall of Tuscarora sandstone. The less daring (but only those sound of wind and limb) can hike to the summit on a 1.3-mile, self-guided trail. The truly sedentary may enjoy the entire spectacle from the restaurant porch of Harper's Old Country Store, a 1902 institution now run by the founder's great-grandson.

The formation, at the virtual center of the Potomac Highlands, provides half the name of the Spruce Knob-Seneca Rocks National Recreation Area, which covers a hefty 100,000 acres within Monongahela National Forest. Spruce Knob, the other half of the title, gets top billing, perhaps because, at 4,861 feet, it is the tallest mountain in the Mountain State. No visitor may claim maximum familiarity with the Highlands without steering up the slopes of Spruce Knob, an ascent that begins at the village of Riverton, just south of Seneca Rocks. At the lower levels are forests of beech, birch, cherry and maple, gradually giving way to mountain ash and red spruce. The last nine miles or so are unpaved; the drive can be rugged in harsh weather, but the reward comes at the summit. Spruces of impossible greenness, lopsided from exposure to endless west winds, spring from the boulder-strewn mountaintop. They line the Whispering Spruce Trail, a ¾-mile interpretive loop around the base of a sturdy stone and steel observation tower, from which the Alleghenies roll away in purple haze like giant frozen waves. Damp white clouds brush past, wetting visitors' faces, a kind of elemental anointing. The entire setting seems mysteriously still, a view from the top of the world, resounding only with the everlasting sigh of the mountain wind.

GRAZING ON THE SODS

For all its drama, the Spruce Knob and Seneca Rocks recreation areas have no monopoly on the Monongahela Forest's rare geology and geography. The Dolly Sods Wilderness Area, a few miles north in Grant and Tucker counties, is a 10,215-acre wilderness with elevations ranging from 2,600 to more than 4,000 feet, creating a climate and plant life comparable to that of northern Canada. Sphagnum bogs, where cranberries grow, heath barrens covered with stunted azaleas and rhododendron, phalanxes of one-sided red spruce and yellow birch, aspens and northern hardwoods are a few exemplars of the plant community. The "sods" of the region's name are open, natural grassy areas, once used by pioneers for grazing stock. Hiking trails and roads traverse part of the most scenic Dolly Sods region, the portion directly on the Allegheny Front; special rules apply to some wilderness areas of heightened environmental importance and sensitivity.

Similarity to Canada is a repeating theme of certain sections of the Potomac Highlands. One part of Webster and Pocahontas counties holds four large bogs that approximate the muskegs of far-northern, often-frozen latitudes. Here at the Monongahela National Forest's Cranberry Glades Botanical Area (part of a larger grouping called the Cranberry Natural Area), a half-mile-long boardwalk leads visitors through two of the bogs, causing no damage to the fragile ecosystem. The

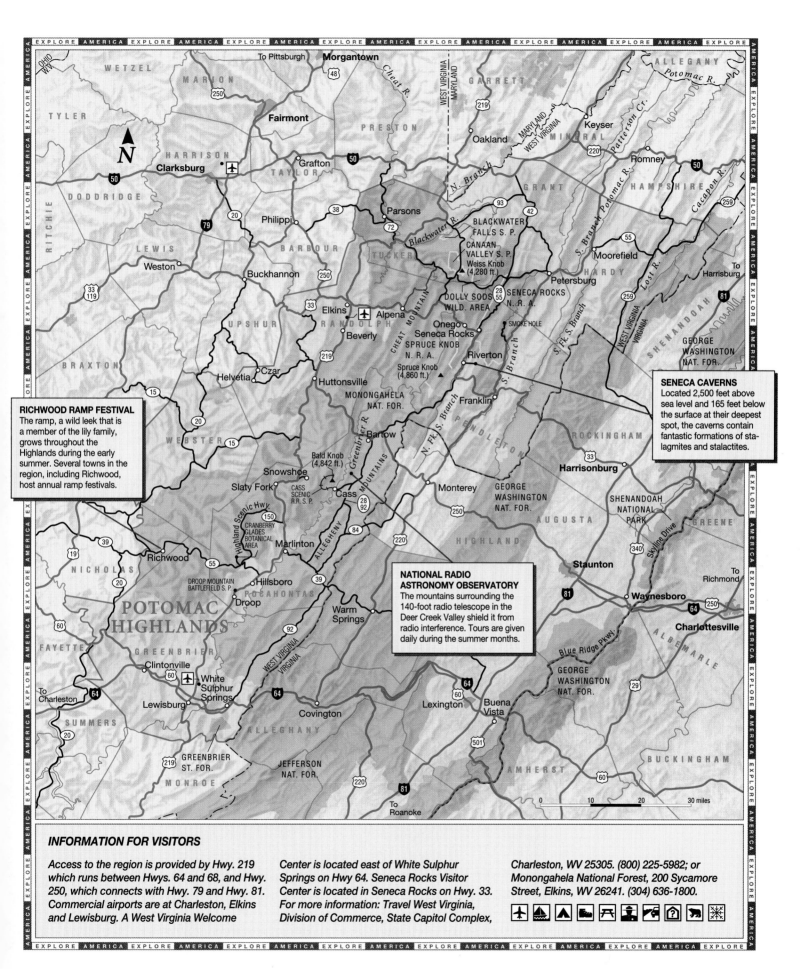

RICHWOOD RAMP FESTIVAL
The ramp, a wild leek that is a member of the lily family, grows throughout the Highlands during the early summer. Several towns in the region, including Richwood, host annual ramp festivals.

SENECA CAVERNS
Located 2,500 feet above sea level and 165 feet below the surface at their deepest spot, the caverns contain fantastic formations of stalagmites and stalactites.

NATIONAL RADIO ASTRONOMY OBSERVATORY
The mountains surrounding the 140-foot radio telescope in the Deer Creek Valley shield it from radio interference. Tours are given daily during the summer months.

POTOMAC HIGHLANDS

0   10   20   30 miles

INFORMATION FOR VISITORS

Access to the region is provided by Hwy. 219 which runs between Hwys. 64 and 68, and Hwy. 250, which connects with Hwy. 79 and Hwy. 81. Commercial airports are at Charleston, Elkins and Lewisburg. A West Virginia Welcome Center is located east of White Sulphur Springs on Hwy 64. Seneca Rocks Visitor Center is located in Seneca Rocks on Hwy. 33. For more information: Travel West Virginia, Division of Commerce, State Capitol Complex, Charleston, WV 25305. (800) 225-5982; or Monongahela National Forest, 200 Sycamore Street, Elkins, WV 26241. (304) 636-1800.

RED AND BLACK

A red fox peeks out of its temporary abode in a hollow log, below. The animal is about the size of a small dog, and feeds on smaller mammals, fruit and grass. This tranquil stretch of the Blackwater River in Canaan Valley, right, flows through marshes and peaty soil, which give the river its color and its name.

ancestors of some plants here moved down in the last ice age, botanists say, and to this day the Cranberry Glades are their southernmost outpost. The cranberry plant itself, a tiny affair growing in sphagnum moss, is hard to see. Not so the bright red oswego tea, orange jewelweed, skunk cabbage, rhododendron and even the snake-mouth orchid.

An air of legends and folklore often clings to the region's natural features. And legends may be disputed: Smoke Hole, a 20-mile gorge carved by the South Branch of the Potomac, was named for the misty atmosphere created by cool air flowing from cave mouths beside the river, Indians smoking their meat or moonshiners tending their stills, depending on who's doing the telling. The most likely explanation, apparently, is the first one. In any case, this superbly beautiful canyon is a favorite for fishermen, kayakers, canoers and wilderness campers.

Intermingled with the vast forests is another major area of natural heritage: The West Virginia State Park System. The state parks offer a more organized plan of activities than the national forests, and some even have the attributes of resorts. Two of them, strikingly different from each other, lie close together in Tucker County, near the dovetail-like border shared with far western Maryland.

THUNDERING
DRAMA

Blackwater Falls State Park centers on the eight-mile-long gorge of the Blackwater River. The water's dark color—more umber than black—is tinted along this stretch by the tannic acid from fallen needles of red spruce and hemlock. At its most dramatic point, the river plunges over a rocky falls five stories high. This thundering show may be seen at close hand from numerous observation points, including stairways and boardwalks ending at the very base of the falls. Up on the rim of the canyon, the park offers accommodation at the rustic Blackwater Lodge. A year-round nature and recreation program includes emphasis on hiking, horseback riding, wildflower study and cross-country skiing.

A few minutes away, in its own ethereal setting of more than 6,000 acres, is Canaan Valley Resort and Conference Center. Canaan (pronounced, with characteristic West Virginia nonconformity, KaNAIN) is another outpost of the Canadian ecosystem, with an average summer high temperature of 75°F. Most of the facilities of this four-season resort are clustered on the valley floor. But this is some valley. It lies at 3,200 feet and is ringed by peaks that rise more than 4,200 feet.

The setting around Canaan's 250-room luxury lodge is a peaceable kingdom of such wild creatures as white-tailed deer, black bear, beaver, fox, wild turkey and assorted waterfowl. The amenities include golf and tennis, but the fame of Canaan probably owes more to its skiing than to warm weather pursuits. Legend has it that as early as the 1940's, airline pilots remarked on the snows down below that lasted long into the spring. Ski enthusiasts from Washington, D.C., came and installed a primitive rope lift in 1952 on Weiss Knob. The same mountain today is served by assorted quadruple and triple chair lifts carrying 6,000 people an hour to 21 slopes and trails. The longest run is 1¼ miles; the vertical drop is 850 feet.

The giant among the region's seven ski areas is Snowshoe, a 10,000-acre complex about 60 miles south, centered on 4,848-foot-high Cheat Mountain in Pocahontas County. With the acquisition of the neighboring Silver Creek Resort in 1992, it solidified its position as the giant of southeastern skiing. The mammoth combined resorts' 50 slopes are dominated by 1½-mile-long Cupp Run, with a 1,500-foot vertical descent. The summit elevation is a mere 18 feet less than Spruce Knob's. Cheat Mountain gets an average 180 inches of snow annually. That and the resort's mighty snowmakers keep 370,000 skiers happy each year.

Even with all this activity, Pocahontas County, like nearly all of the Potomac Highlands, retains its ancient remoteness, and a drive almost anywhere in the region—especially in winter—offers a peaceful isolation that is rare in the Middle Atlantic states. With the hardwood forests bare of foliage, the winter landscape opens wide with heart-catching vistas. If snow is on the ground, a common thing between December and March, the white contours of mountains, ridges and fields stand out like wrinkles on a cosmic counterpane. Ten-foot-long icicles hang from roadside cliffs. Angus cattle stand motionless in white meadows, their heads lowered against the wind. Sculpted snowdrifts curl along the banks of streams, and the bare branches

MAPLE MAGIC
An orange-leaved sugar maple tree in the Canaan Valley State Park heralds the end of summer. The sap in the trees rises in the early spring when traditional maple syrup production begins; about 45 gallons of sap boil down to one gallon of golden syrup.

of distant trees soften the scene's austerity with lacy taupe shadows.

But some of the most striking panoramas become chancy in winter. The road up Spruce Knob is often closed, as is another special drive called the Highland Scenic Highway, or Route 150. The latter, much easier on a motor vehicle in any season, is a fully paved, 23-mile-long loop near the town of Marlinton. Views of range after range of mountain wilderness unfold where not even a small farm interrupts the pristine forest. More than 60 percent of the loop is above 4,000 feet.

Thus on every hand the rugged geography molds a singular landscape, creating in turn a natural history that became inextricably mingled with human history. The wild topography helped defeat—of all people—General Robert E. Lee in his first campaign of the Civil War, a confused, doomed 1861 effort to consolidate Confederate ventures west of the Alleghenies. (Much of this activity is noted in historical markers along Highway 219.) The campaign was not a total loss for Lee: It was here that he purchased his famous war-horse, Traveller. Two years later, the Southerners took another shellacking at Droop Mountain in Pocahontas County. Rebel strength in the region was wrecked, and the Highland's counties became part of the new, pro-Union state of West Virginia.

Like the Civil War, unrestrained lumbering laid a heavy hand on the region. Yet, as with the war, those days too are long gone. At Cass Scenic Railroad State Park, the railroad that once hauled loads of chained-down logs now carries festive passengers through the rare mountain flora as ancient steam locomotives puff their way up the flanks of

BATTLEFIELD REVISITED
The last and bloodiest Civil War battle on West Virginia soil took place on a high mountain plateau overlooking the Greenbrier Valley. Reenactments of the battle take place every other fall at the Droop Mountain Battlefield State Park; a lookout tower provides sweeping views of the valley.

Bald Knob, West Virginia's second-highest peak. In Cass itself, a virtually intact company town of 1902, guests may stay in authentic logging company cabins, or in the former superintendent's house.

Marlinton, county seat of Pocahontas, straddles the broad and sparkling Greenbrier River, perhaps the Highlands' choicest setting. It also retains a sturdy vigor in its turn-of-the century downtown, including a National Register railroad depot of 1901. Marlinton's Pioneer Days Festival is a popular July event.

FESTIVALS
TO CELEBRATE
HERITAGE

Still older times are recalled by the town of Beverly, where the Randolph County Historical Society Museum traces the county's 200-year history in a store building of 1828, the People's Cash and Trade Store. Nearby (and much larger) Elkins, seat of Randolph, stages the notable Mountain State Forest Festival in October and the Augusta Heritage Arts Workshops at Davis and Elkins College in July and August. Travelers dedicated to finding the remotest town in the Highlands should consider Helvetia, founded by Swiss immigrants. Ten historic buildings, and folklore festivals such as *Fasnacht* and the Helvetia Fair, keep the heritage alive. In tidy, archaic-looking little Hillsboro, visitors drop by the old green-fronted Hillsboro Country Store (groceries,

antiques and feed) and the Gothic revival house where the great novelist Pearl Buck was born. Antebellum Moorefield, another county seat, is the centerpiece of Hardy County Heritage Weekend each September, a time to tour many of the region's historic homes along the Potomac's South Branch.

Greenbrier County, whose landscape opens wider than most, enjoys a unique role in trans-Allegheny chronicles. And, of all the region's towns, Lewisburg might be called a special case. Legendary frontiersman Andrew Lewis first explored the site in 1751. Settlers built a fort beside a spring Lewis used, and hung on to defeat the fearsome Shawnee, ancient proprietors of the fertile, game-rich region.

By the Revolution's end, Lewisburg was thriving at its strategic crossroads location on the Midland Trail (a great east-west turnpike of frontier days, corresponding to today's Highways 60 and 64) and the Seneca Trail (today's Highway 219, heading north into the Potomac Highlands' remoter reaches). In the prosperous 1830's and '40's, handsome brick mansions with great white pillars rose along Lewisburg's hilly streets. When the Civil War came, a downtown battle raged through the street in front of the 1837 courthouse. It was a bloody affair, but the courthouse survived.

Today's visitor finds a jewel of a town whose National Register Historic District holds more than 60 significant 18th- and 19th-century buildings. One is the General Lewis Inn of 1834, a long-popular hostelry crammed with area antiques. The town is a popular antiques market. The local speech seems softer and more Southern than the prevailing mountain twang. Such clues uncover a cultural vein that runs straight back from Greenbrier County to Old Virginia.

Nowhere is the vein richer than eight miles east of Lewisburg at White Sulphur Springs and the resort called The Greenbrier. As pure and white and perfectly decorated as an Olympian wedding cake, the great 650-room hotel rests lightly in its 6,500 acres of golf courses, tennis courts, stables, gardens and rows of elegant cottages, a sort of recreational promised land, ineffably glamorous, a center of taste, fashion and good living still going strong after two centuries. Yet, with almost offhand ease, this favorite retreat of princes and presidents still presents the same air of democratic friendliness that pervades the region. It is a creature of its place here in the mountains, and in the words of Lord Byron, "High mountains are a feeling." Whether in the pink-and-white magnificence of The Greenbrier's dining room or on the Front Porch Restaurant at Harper's Old Country Store in Seneca Rocks, the feeling touches the same human chords. Hospitality. Directness. Unpretentious warmth. Other regions should be so fortunate.

Nearby Sites & Attractions

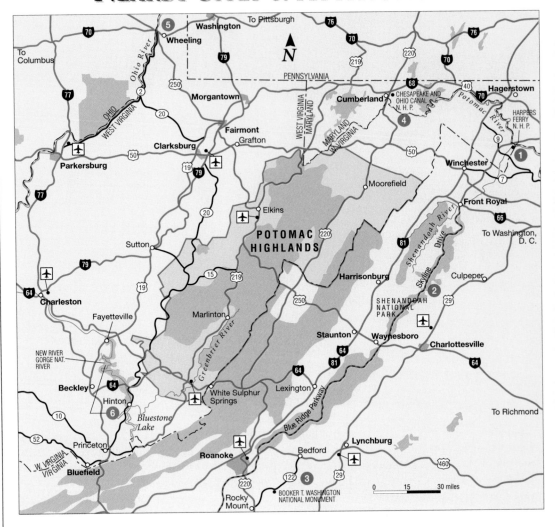

The South River Falls Trail in Shenandoah National Park provides hikers with spectacular views of the South River Falls, seen here surrounded by brilliant fall foliage.

① HARPERS FERRY NATIONAL HISTORICAL PARK

Located in the Blue Ridge Mountains at the confluence of the Shenandoah and Potomac Rivers, Harpers Ferry was the location of John Brown's famous raid on the federal armory during the night of October 16, 1859. The ardent abolitionist's attack on the town brought the subject of slavery to the attention of the nation 16 months before the start of the Civil War. During the summer, costumed interpreters, dressed as shopkeepers and homeowners, reenact the days when the town was occupied by soldiers. The Appalachian Trail runs through the park; a less strenuous trail follows the Chesapeake and Ohio Canal towpath. Fishing, rafting and rock climbing are other popular activities. Located on Hwy. 340, northeast of Front Royal.

② SHENANDOAH NATIONAL PARK

The park's 195,403 acres encompass tranquil forests of balsam, hemlock, spruce, oak, pine, maple and hickory trees that drape the slopes of the Blue Ridge Mountains. Shenandoah's forests, rocky hollows and streams are home to 1,200 species of plants, 200 types of birds and countless reptiles, amphibians, fish and insects. The 105-mile Skyline Drive runs in a northeast-southwest direction and most of the park's 500 miles of hiking trails are accessible from the route, including a portion of the Appalachian Trail. Many lookout points along Skyline Drive provide magnificent views of the Shenandoah Valley. Skyline Drive runs between the Rockfish Gap entrance (near Waynesboro) and the town of Front Royal.

③ BOOKER T. WASHINGTON NATIONAL MONUMENT

Booker T. Washington was born into slavery on April 5, 1856, on a tobacco farm in Virginia. When the Civil War ended, he was freed and given the opportunity to attend the Hampton Institute. He did so well at school that he was recommended as the head of a new school for blacks, to be called the Tuskegee Institute. The National Monument includes a reconstruction of Washington's boyhood home, a one-room log cabin with a dirt floor and white-washed walls. The owner's house, smokehouse, blacksmith's shed, tobacco barn and horse barn are some of the other buildings on the site. Costumed craftspeople reenact the workaday life of black slaves on a tobacco farm prior to the Civil War. Several hiking trails wend their way through the 204-acre site. Located 22 miles southeast of Roanoke on Hwy. 122.

④ CHESAPEAKE AND OHIO CANAL NATIONAL HISTORICAL PARK

The 184-mile C&O Canal stretches alongside the Potomac River from Georgetown in Washington, D.C., to Cumberland in western Maryland. Seventy-four locks raise the water level from sea level to an elevation of 605 feet. Work on the waterway began in 1828 and took 22 years to complete. By that time, railroads had made canal transport obsolete. However, the C&O remained a busy transportation route until 1924. Mule-drawn canal barges manned by costumed crew members take visitors on trips from mid-April to mid-October. Some sections of the canal are also open for boating and canoeing. The 12-foot-wide towpath is popular with joggers, hikers and cyclists. Horseback riding is permitted between Swains Lock and Cumberland. There are 45 access points to the park.

⑤ WHEELING

The town of Wheeling stands on the site of Fort Henry, built around 1774 to protect the fledgling settlement from Indian attack. Following the American Revolution, the town prospered as a center of trade and industry and a gateway for west-ward-bound pioneers. Wheeling's Independence Hall was the setting for West Virginia's declaration of independence from Virginia in 1861, and the town served as the new state's first capital. A walking tour of the Victorian district allows visitors to admire Wheeling's 67 historic homes and buildings. These include Centre Market Square, originally a farmer's market, and Chapline Street Row, a group of townhouses owned by Wheeling's bankers and mill owners. The Wheeling Suspension Bridge, the first bridge to span the Ohio River, was built in 1849. At the time, it was the longest single span suspension bridge in the world. Located on Hwy. 70.

⑥ NEW RIVER GORGE NATIONAL RIVER

The New River has flowed along its present course for more than 65 million years, making it one of the oldest rivers in the world. In the process, it has carved a deep gorge in the surrounding rock. The park's 62,000 acres preserve a 53-mile stretch of the New River as it surges northward to join the Ohio. The river is a paradise for whitewater rafters, but also offers placid stretches ideal for canoeing and fishing. Along the shore are a number of once-booming coal mining towns, now abandoned, which sprang up in the 1870's after the construction of the Chesapeake and Ohio Railroad. Visitors can travel the entire length of the gorge within the park aboard a regular-service Amtrak train. Outside Fayetteville, the New River Gorge Bridge provides a spectacular view of the gorge, and the river—876 feet below. Completed in 1977, the bridge is the longest single arch steel span in the world, and the second highest in the U.S. The Canyon Rim Visitor Center, on Hwy. 19, offers superb views of the bridge and the gorge. There are two other visitor centers: one near Hinton, on Hwy. 20, and the other near Beckley, north of Hwy. 64.

Independence Hall in Wheeling served as West Virginia's first state capitol. This finely restored Renaissance Revival building, which also did duty as the town's custom house, post office and federal court, is now a museum with exhibits on West Virginia's cultural heritage.

Visitors can get an overview of Harpers Ferry National Historical Park from Louden Heights. Because the strategic location of the town made it a military target throughout the Civil War, Harpers Ferry changed hands many times. A 19th-century blacksmith's shop, a tavern and a dry-goods store are among some of the buildings that are open to the public.

HIDDEN VALLEYS

Wisconsin's Hidden Valleys share their secrets with soaring eagles and intrepid travelers alike.

The solitary bald eagle is a winged dot against the blue skies, first soaring toward the ragged clouds and then swooping downward toward the maple- and oak-forested ridges of southwestern Wisconsin. Far below the bird, the coffee-colored Mississippi River rolls southward, its swift current hard and cold as new steel. The eagle, with its five-foot wingspan, expertly rides the sweet air currents above the bluffs.

Here, in a tiny chunk of Grant, Crawford and Iowa Counties, lies the heart of the Hidden Valleys of Wisconsin, a countryside tailor-made for eagles...and for explorers. And although the roadbound traveler doesn't have the advantage of the eagle's lofty viewpoint, the secrets of the Hidden Valleys are uncovered in other ways—by hiking along a shady creek, or by munching a freshly picked apple bought from a farmer's roadside stall.

A number of river frontage county roads and highways crisscross the area, exposing all the counties' charm—a delightful mix of farmland,

lost villages, monuments and German communities where folks say "zink" instead of "sink." Some of the treasures waiting to be explored include the town of Muscoda (the state's Morel Mushroom Capital), Richland Center (birthplace of the architect Frank Lloyd Wright), Boscobel (the Turkey Hunting Capital), the orchard country of Gays Mills, and Soldiers Grove—America's first solar-powered village. Highways have their place if a traveler is in a hurry. But miss a turn in the Hidden Valleys and adventure will beckon down rural roads named Squirrel Hollow, Closing Dam, Far-Nuf, Dog-tail and Hippy Hollow. And don't bypass Archie's Lane.

THE DRIFTLESS AREA

The reason the valleys retain their flavor of remoteness has to do with their geological formation. When ancient oceans covered the Mississippi River Valley some 300-600 million years ago, sediments settling on the ocean floor eventually formed layers of sandstone and limestone. When the oceans disappeared, rivers and streams went to work eroding these layers into the steep bluffs, ridges and shady valleys that characterize the landscape of the Hidden Valleys. Although glaciers scoured and leveled most of the landscape of what is now Wisconsin, the ice sheets bypassed the southwestern corner of the state. Geographers call this region the "driftless area," because of the lack of "drift" (rock debris) left behind when the ice sheets melted. What remains is an ancient landscape of surprising variety and brooding grandeur. The farmers who raise crops and dairy cattle on the valley bottoms can testify to the exceptional fertility of their soils. And through it all courses the mighty Mississippi River.

But the Hidden Valleys contain the story of people as well as geography. At least 12,000 years ago, nomadic Paleo-Indians wandered across these bluffs. They were followed by other cultures: the Effigy Builders, for instance, who favored bears and birds as sacred totems, lived in the area until about A.D. 1300. They constructed the huge, animal-shaped burial mounds visible today at Effigy Mounds National Monument on the Iowa side of the Mississippi.

In more recent times, the Hidden Valleys were home to other temporary residents: the Sauk, Fox, Sioux, Winnebago, Potawatomi, Menominee and other Native Americans. Kickapoo Indian Caverns, discovered in the early 1800's, once sheltered local Indians and ranks as the largest cave system in the state. Wisconsin's many rivers and lakes favored water transport, and the canoe fleets of these tribes turned the rivers into veritable superhighways.

In the 1600's French traders and missionaries set up a chain of trading posts and forts from Québec to Green Bay. They had heard tales of the Mississippi and were eager to find this "Father of Waters." In 1673, the 28-year-old adventurer Louis Jolliet traveled south along the Wisconsin River in the company of Father Jacques Marquette and a number of Indian guides. The party arrived at the confluence of the Wisconsin and the Mississippi on June 17, 1673. From Marquette's description, historians have concluded that the men were in

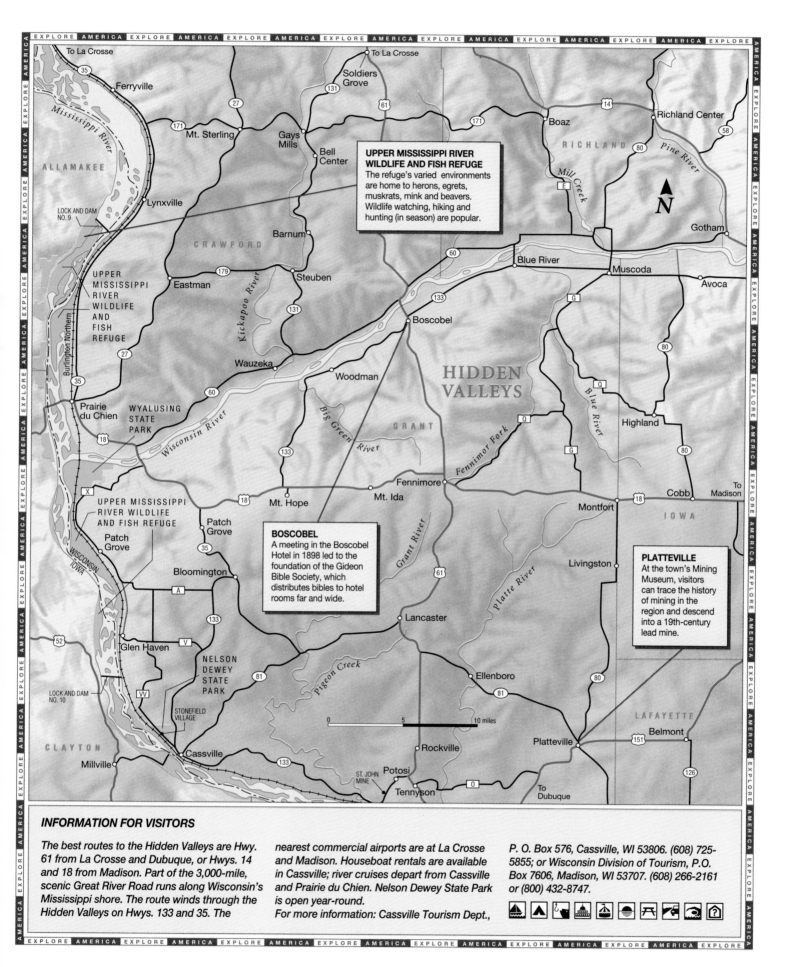

UPPER MISSISSIPPI RIVER WILDLIFE AND FISH REFUGE
The refuge's varied environments are home to herons, egrets, muskrats, mink and beavers. Wildlife watching, hiking and hunting (in season) are popular.

HIDDEN VALLEYS

BOSCOBEL
A meeting in the Boscobel Hotel in 1898 led to the foundation of the Gideon Bible Society, which distributes bibles to hotel rooms far and wide.

PLATTEVILLE
At the town's Mining Museum, visitors can trace the history of mining in the region and descend into a 19th-century lead mine.

0   5   10 miles

INFORMATION FOR VISITORS

The best routes to the Hidden Valleys are Hwy. 61 from La Crosse and Dubuque, or Hwys. 14 and 18 from Madison. Part of the 3,000-mile, scenic Great River Road runs along Wisconsin's Mississippi shore. The route winds through the Hidden Valleys on Hwys. 133 and 35. The nearest commercial airports are at La Crosse and Madison. Houseboat rentals are available in Cassville; river cruises depart from Cassville and Prairie du Chien. Nelson Dewey State Park is open year-round.

For more information: Cassville Tourism Dept., P. O. Box 576, Cassville, WI 53806. (608) 725-5855; or Wisconsin Division of Tourism, P.O. Box 7606, Madison, WI 53707. (608) 266-2161 or (800) 432-8747.

the vicinity of what is today the city of Prairie du Chien, the heart of Crawford County. This was the first record of Europeans on the Upper Mississippi.

Marquette recorded that he entered the river "with a joy that I cannot express." Today's visitor can get the same feeling, standing at dawn beside the Father Marquette statue in Prairie du Chien. Regardless of the season, the sun first shyly peeks over the horizon, and then comes on with an explosive drumroll. Almost immediately, the rough scenery stands to attention, bathed in fabulous light. The stone priest, hands outward, seems to welcome the day.

It wasn't long before other explorers and traders followed Father Marquette: Daniel Greysolon Duluth, Boisguillot, the Marin family, La Salle, Nicholas Perrot, Pierre LeSueur and the *coureurs de bois*—those hardy trappers who moved through the wild valleys like ghosts. A rough wooden trading fort was built by the French as early as 1689 at the strategic confluence of the Wisconsin and Mississippi Rivers. Following the French came the British and the Yankees—brawling over the furs and the lead, both found in abundance in the neighborhood. Settlers and miners flooded in during the 1830's, for a brief time making southwestern Wisconsin more heavily populated than early Chicago and Milwaukee.

Present-day residents of the Hidden Valleys have a long tie to the past, some as far back as French days. Many area farms have been in the same families since a generation before the Civil War. This attachment to land and home provides a permanence to the entire region. But life is slowly changing in Hidden Valleys. The population of Grant County, for example, shrank by five percent

between 1980 and 1990. And agriculture is losing its edge as the primary source of income. Tourism has become a strong, complementary business to manufacturing and the service industries that are gradually taking over the economic lead from cattle and corn.

FIRST IMPRESSIONS COUNT	The friendly welcoming signs at the outskirts of some communities were an outgrowth of a program known as First

Impressions, which sends volunteers from one community to visit a neighboring town and grade its appearance. Even tiny Woodman (population 120), tucked into a bend of the Wisconsin River, now boasts one of these cheery howdy-do's. Most of the signs were painted by a local craftsman, who traded his handiwork for two open lots in the village on which to build his new house. Exchanges like this are typical of life in the Hidden Valleys.

Prairie du Chien ("Prairie of the Dog") was named by French-Canadian trappers for a Mesquakie chief whose name translates as "dog," or *chien* in French. The city annually celebrates its 300 years as a trading center with a rendezvous of buckskinners in period costumes on Father's Day weekend. As the second-oldest settlement in

Wisconsin (only Green Bay is older), Prairie du Chien capitalizes on its other long-ago connections at Villa Louis, opulent home of the Dousman family and today a state historical site. Hercules Dousman was an agent for John Jacob Astor's American Fur Company. He earned millions from the fur trade, and from shrewd investments in the lumber and railroad industries. Dousman built his house on St. Feriole Island, atop an old Indian ceremonial mound. In 1868, his widow demolished the original house and hired a Milwaukee architect to build a brand new one for her.

At Fort Crawford Medical Museum (housed in the restored fort's former hospital), Dr. William Beaumont continued the landmark experiments on human digestion that he had begun at Fort Mackinac in 1822. Fort Crawford was also where a young Jefferson Davis courted the daughter of Zachary Taylor.

One of the best adventures in any season is the roughly four-mile stretch of Dugway Road between Bagley and the hamlet of Glen Haven. On the left of the one-lane gravel road are sheer limestone cliffs; on the right is a steep embankment that rolls down to the Burlington Northern Railroad tracks, seemingly inches from the edge of the Mississippi River below. Hunters of elusive, exotic ginseng scurry around these woods in the autumn, search-

VICTORIAN VILLA

Villa Louis in Prairie du Chien was built by the widow of Wisconsin's first millionaire, fur trader Hercules Dousman. Now a museum, the house contains a fine collection of Victorian decorative arts, as well as displays chronicling the history of western Wisconsin.

ing for the fabled herb's telltale compound leaves, red berries and human-shaped roots. Just south of the mouth of the Wisconsin River is Wyalusing State Park. Its 500-foot bluffs provide superb views of the Mississippi, and the park contains numerous burial mounds raised by ancient Indian cultures.

From Glen Haven, called Stumptown in its old-time riverfront days, the road snakes on into the quiet river town of Cassville. A nine-car ferry operates in season across the Mississippi from Cassville to Turkey River Landing on the Iowa side. Residents of Cassville laughingly refer to the neighboring state as the "boonies." Since 1929, with a hiatus from 1945 to 1961, the town's Twin-O-Rama each July brings together twins from around the country for a double-your-fun celebration.

Near Cassville, County Road VV bisects the Nelson Dewey State Park, named after Wisconsin's first governor, who built a house called Stonefield atop the bluffs here. On the flatlands along the

VALLEY VISTA
A stone barn near the town of Gays Mills speaks of the region's ties to the land. This is apple country, and every year the town celebrates with spring and fall festivals.

EAGLE'S-EYE VIEW
Stonefield Village in Nelson Dewey State Park takes its name from a house built on the Mississippi bluffs by Wisconsin's first governor. The view from the heights reveals a tidy 1890's farming village, complete with railroad.

58

Mississippi lies Stonefield Village, a replica community of the 1890's, featuring shops, a school, a blacksmith, a railroad depot and the State Agricultural Museum. Climb the bluffs for a view of the river, and a chance to observe the area's rich bird life. In winter, lucky visitors can witness the unforgettable sight of migrating bald eagles swooping down to the river in search of fish.

THE BADGER STATE

Lead miners put Potosi on the map as early as the late 1600's, but the area's lead deposits had been worked by Native Americans well before European settlers came on the scene. Fighting off rattlesnakes and claim jumpers, the first miners lived in burrows high in the hills. Their crude homes looked like badger holes, and hence the name of "Badger State" for Wisconsin. The Hidden Valleys produced most of the lead shot used during the Civil War. The St.

John Mine in Potosi is open for tours from May through October. Miners' chisel marks are still visible on the shaft walls.

Potosi's nearly four-mile-long main street has been called the longest of its kind in America. The road, which connects ghost communities such as British Hollow, has no intersections because of the steep cliffs that line the long, narrow valley. The nearby hamlet of Tennyson is another of the many communities born during Wisconsin's "lead rush."

The red-granite Grant County Courthouse in Lancaster has a glass and copper dome modeled after St. Peter's Basilica in Rome. The courthouse square is also the site of the nation's first official Civil War monument, dedicated on July 4, 1867. The memorial is inscribed with the names of the 755 Grant County soldiers who died or were injured during the war between the states. On the southeast corner of the square is a statue of the aforementioned Governor Dewey, who is buried amid the weather-beaten tombstones in a tiny cemetery between the First Presbyterian and Emmanuel Episcopal Churches at Jefferson and Walnut Streets.

A stop in Fennimore demonstrates the vibrancy of southwestern Wisconsin's small towns. A giant statue of Igor the friendly mouse stands outside the Fennimore Cheese plant, just one of the region's many cheese producers. The town's determination and pride in its heritage are shown to best advantage in Fennimore's narrow-gauge train, tagged "The Dinky." The 1907 Davenport locomotive is now proudly displayed, after being saved from a salvage yard wrecker's torch. A state historical marker and a small park on the north side of town are now home for the little locomotive, which operated from 1878 to 1926 on a 16-mile rail line. Volunteer townsfolk have built a museum themselves to house railroad artifacts.

Fennimore's back roads and countryside offer many treasures just waiting to be enjoyed. Smooth ribbons of highway give way to winding rustic roads that beckon the motorist to enjoy a leisurely drive through scenic broad valleys. More than 100 miles of spring-fed trout streams offer superlative fishing, while the surrounding countryside serves as a habitat for deer, wild turkey, grouse and a wide array of birds. A stop at Fennimore's 45-acre Oakwood Nature Park offers a glimpse of native trees and wildflowers as well as wilderness camping.

So between nature's beauty, statues of mice, priests, explorers and bearded politicians, eagle-watching, tractors and freshly plowed fields, sun-burned farmfolks and crossroads villages, the inquisitive traveler can quite easily unlock the secrets of the Hidden Valleys. In fact, it's a delightful experience just turning the key.

STUDY IN SCARLET
Sunset and the onset of fall turn an ivy-wreathed oak tree into a creation worthy of an artist's palette. Deciduous trees such as hickory, maple and oak are typical of the forests of southwestern Wisconsin.

NEARBY SITES & ATTRACTIONS

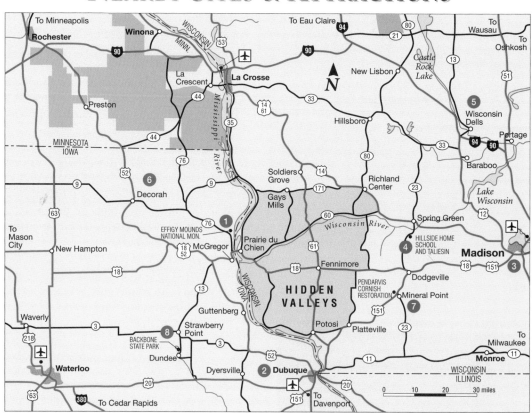

Architect Frank Lloyd Wright lived most of his life on a 600-acre estate near Spring Green. Wright named his house Taliesin (a Welsh word meaning "Shining Brow"). The architect included the layout of the grounds, above, in his overall design. The Taliesin complex, right, also served as a progressive boarding school.

① EFFIGY MOUNDS NATIONAL MONUMENT

Burial and ceremonial mounds, 191 of them, believed to date from 500 B.C., are preserved at this national monument, which also includes 1,487 acres of parkland. Huge earthworks in the shape of birds in flight and bears are the most striking of the mounds. The oldest, linear and conical in formation, were created by members of the Red Ocher culture. Hiking trails link the mounds and hug the bluffs of the Mississippi River, providing visitors with spectacular views. This area is on the path of the Mississippi Flyway, and bald eagles and ospreys may be spotted during spring and fall migration. Visitors can learn more about this unique historical site at the visitor center, where artifacts are on display; film and slide presentations are also shown. Located on Hwy. 76.

② DUBUQUE

Iowa's oldest city, situated on the banks of the Mississippi River, boasts a number of historically significant buildings. The gold-domed brick courthouse, with its 200-foot tower, and the city jail are both examples of Egyptian Revival architecture. The courthouse now houses an art museum. At the Woodward Riverboat Museum, located on the waterfront in the historic Ice Harbor, visitors can climb aboard a scale model of a paddlewheel riverboat. Mathias Ham House Museum, an elegant stone mansion built in 1856, is furnished with antiques; a log cabin and a schoolhouse are situated on the grounds. The Dubuque Arboretum is open year-round. Located on Hwys. 52, 61 and 20.

③ MADISON

Wisconsin's capital city is located on a narrow isthmus between Mendota and Monona lakes. The skyline of the city is dominated by the Wisconsin State Capitol, an imposing white granite structure in Classical Revival style. The University of Wisconsin was established here in 1848. Today, the 903-acre university campus stretches for more than two miles along the south shore of Lake Mendota. During the summer months, Capitol Square is the site of the lively Dane County Farmers' Market. Wisconsin's State Historical Museum, located on Capitol Square, exhibits artifacts pertaining to prehistoric Indian culture, as well as more contemporary aspects of Wisconsin's varied past. Observatory and Willow

Drives offer motorists scenic views of Mendota and Monona lakes. Located on Hwys. 90, 94 and 151.

4 HILLSIDE HOME SCHOOL AND TALIESIN

Perhaps the most innovative architect of the 20th century, Frank Lloyd Wright was born in Wisconsin and lived most of his life on a 600-acre estate in the Wisconsin River Valley. Hillside Home School, one of the first co-educational boarding schools in the U.S., was run by Wright's two aunts, Jane and Nell Lloyd Jones, from 1886-1917. Wright added buildings to the school in 1898 and 1902, which now house the Frank Lloyd Wright School of Architecture. Taliesin, the architect's home from 1911, has an exceptional view of the Mississippi River. Visitors can tour the house, where Wright worked and entertained with his third wife, Olgivanna Milannof, as well as the surrounding estate. Located 3 miles south of Spring Green on Hwy. 23.

5 WISCONSIN DELLS

These layered sandstone monoliths, jutting high above the waters of the Wisconsin River, took shape millions of years ago. Before the Ice Ages, the area lay at the bottom of a vast sea; sand on the seabed gradually hardened into rock, which was later ground by glaciers and carved by the Wisconsin River. Boat tours provide visitors with awesome views of these unique rock formations, sandstone cliffs and grassy canyons; a complete tour of the Upper and Lower Dells takes about 3½ hours. Other sights in the area include the Wisconsin Deer Park, a 28-acre wildlife park; and the H.H. Bennet Foundation Museum, built in 1865, and the oldest photographic studio in the country. Located a mile east of Hwy. 90/94.

6 DECORAH

Decorah is a picturesque Norwegian-American town situated close to the banks of the Upper Iowa River—one of the state's wildest waterways. Vesterheim, a Norwegian-American museum, has a large collection of Norwegian folk art and 15 historic buildings, including two Norwegian pioneer homes, a church and a three-story gristmill. An 1850 farmstead and a country church are located 7 miles southeast of Decorah. Located on Hwys. 9 and 52.

7 MINERAL POINT

During the early 1830's, lead deposits in this area attracted settlers from New England, the southern states and as far away as Cornwall, England. The Cornish miners, known as "Cousin Jacks," built houses that still stand today. Visitors can tour six of these log-and-limestone homes at The Pendarvis Cornish Restoration, as well as enjoy a nature walk through 40 acres in the old mining area, where prairie grasses and wildflowers now grow. A number of galleries display works by local artists. Joseph Guntry House, a Victorian home, is located near Mineral Point and contains exhibits on the history

of the area. Located 50 miles southwest of Madison on Hwy. 151.

8 BACKBONE STATE PARK

This beautiful 1,750-acre state park takes its name from the high ridge of rock that has vertebrae-like boulders running along its spine. The ridge, the most precipitous faces of which are popular with rock climbers, is almost a quarter of a mile long. Four miles of hiking trails follow the banks of the Maquoketa River, where wild geraniums and prairie grass grow, and wind-blown cedar and pine cover the upper ridges. The Maquoketa, which virtually surrounds Backbone State Park, has been dammed to create an 85-acre lake that is ideal for boating and fishing. Located 45 miles east of Waterloo off Hwy. 3.

Norwegian immigrants settled eastern Iowa in large numbers during the 19th century. The Vesterheim Museum in Decorah celebrates this northern heritage with displays of costumes, furniture, interiors and household items. The wall-hanging cupboard, shown at left, was built around 1833 in the Telemark region of southern Norway, and decorated with rosemaling (painted floral designs in Scandinavian peasant style).

One of the highlights of the interior of the Wisconsin State Capitol building in Madison is its domed ceiling. The dome is the second highest in the U.S.

CAJUN COUNTRY

---

*Son-of-a-gun, we'll have big fun
on the bayou . . . so goes the popular
song that celebrates Cajun life.*

Just how the Cajun culture of South Louisiana
evolved into one of storied gaiety and good
nature is a mystery as puzzling as any held by the
swamps and marshes that sustain it. But the
descendants of the French-speaking, devoutly
Catholic settlers, driven from their homes in
Acadia (in what is now eastern Canada) nearly
250 years ago, have carved out a peaceful—even
mirthful—coexistence with their tortured history and special environment. *Laissez les bons temps
rouler* seems to be the motto of Acadiana. Let the
good times roll.

From music to food to language, Cajun
Country—a triangular expanse of lowland that
stretches along the Gulf Coast from the
Mississippi River to Texas and tapers to a point on
Saline Lake, east of Alexandria—is virtually a
nation unto itself, holding hard to its history and
customs and celebrating the soggy earth's bounty of odd creatures and vegetation. Since arriving in the southern United States, Cajuns—the
word is a corruption of Acadians—have clung to

Oak Alley is one of the grand plantations lining the Great River Road that runs the 80 miles from New Orleans to Baton Rouge. Plantations once sat cheek by jowl along the Mississippi; the river was the highway for their cotton and sugar crops.

HOLLY BEACH
Nicknamed the "Cajun Riviera," it is the longest beach in Louisiana and a good spot for swimming, fishing and birdwatching.

INFORMATION FOR VISITORS

Hwy. 10 traverses Cajun Country in a west-east direction, connecting Lake Charles, Lafayette, Baton Rouge and New Orleans. Hwys. 49 and 90 run in a north-south direction through the heart of the region, linking Lafayette, New Iberia, Morgan City and Houma. Smaller roads crisscross the

---

their language and their religion and resisted assimilation like no other cultural or linguistic minority in the country. There are nearly half a million Cajuns in this region who speak French either as a primary or secondary language, and some who do not speak fluent English. Here, individuals of Anglo descent still may be referred to as *les Américains.* Even so, the Cajuns have happily adapted to the pace of modern America without sacrificing any of their renowned *joie de vivre.*

The ancestors of the Cajuns were the French colonists who settled on the rich farmland around the Bay of Fundy, in what are now the Canadian provinces of New Brunswick and Nova Scotia, during the 1600's. They called their new home *Acadie.* The tides of war soon swept over the region, and Acadia, as the English called it, came under British control in 1713. In 1755, British authorities demanded that the Acadians swear an oath of allegiance to the British crown. The Acadians refused, and were expelled from their lands in a mass deportation known as *Le Grand Dérangement.*

The exiles were scattered to the American colonies, to England and back to Europe. Some found themselves as far afield as the West Indies, French Guiana and the Falkland Islands. After years of wandering, a few hundred Acadians reached Louisiana. But Louisiana had been ceded from French hands to Spanish in 1762, and the Acadians, once again outcasts, were offered land grants west of the Mississippi. If they were willing to settle it.

Overleaf: The rising sun lights up a handpainted barn in Carencro, just outside of Lafayette in the heart of Cajun Country.

64

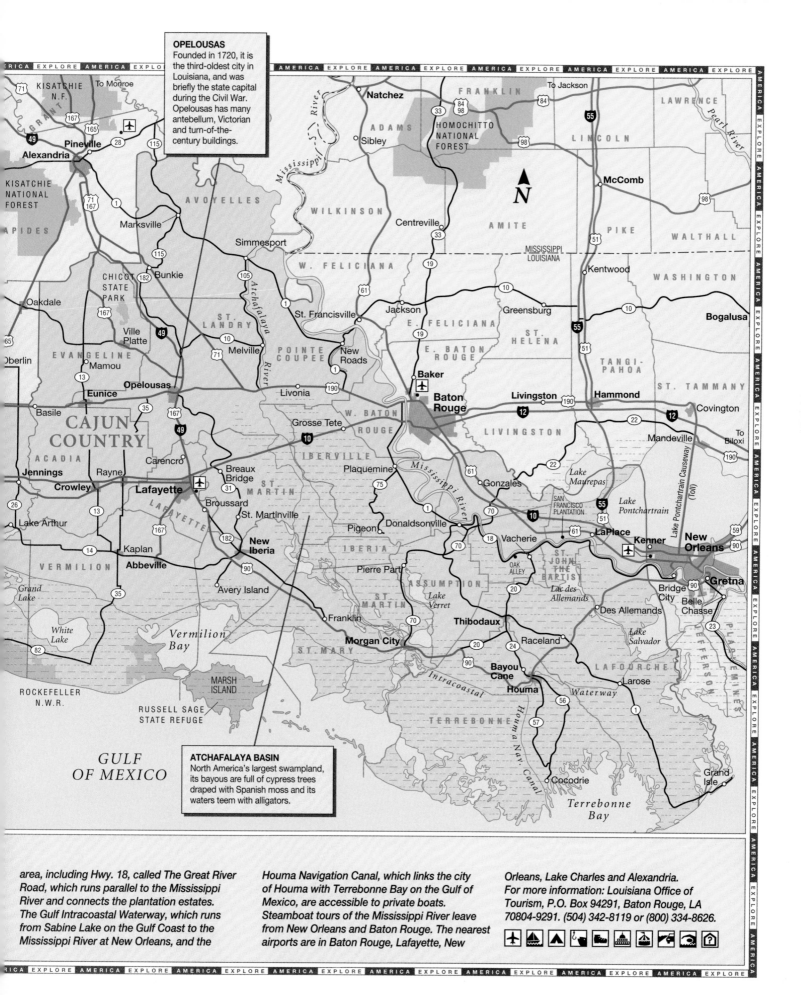

OPELOUSAS
Founded in 1720, it is the third-oldest city in Louisiana, and was briefly the state capital during the Civil War. Opelousas has many antebellum, Victorian and turn-of-the-century buildings.

ATCHAFALAYA BASIN
North America's largest swampland, its bayous are full of cypress trees draped with Spanish moss and its waters teem with alligators.

area, including Hwy. 18, called *The Great River Road*, which runs parallel to the Mississippi River and connects the plantation estates. The Gulf Intracoastal Waterway, which runs from Sabine Lake on the Gulf Coast to the Mississippi River at New Orleans, and the

Houma Navigation Canal, which links the city of Houma with Terrebonne Bay on the Gulf of Mexico, are accessible to private boats. Steamboat tours of the Mississippi River leave from New Orleans and Baton Rouge. The nearest airports are in Baton Rouge, Lafayette, New

Orleans, Lake Charles and Alexandria.
For more information: Louisiana Office of Tourism, P.O. Box 94291, Baton Rouge, LA 70804-9291. (504) 342-8119 or (800) 334-8626.

The portrait of a young lady, right, seems to watch over Parlange Plantation. The plantation is still in operation and has remained in the same family for almost 250 years. A French settler in the 18th century planted 28 oak trees leading from the river to his modest home. Now the quarter-mile alley of oaks leads to Oak Alley, a Creole-Greek house with 28 columns and magnificent galleries, below.

It was a place that seemed fit mostly for trappers and hermits, a region of raging rivers, languid streams, fields of muck and patches of habitable soil accessible mostly by shallow boat. Rainfall from as far north as Canada, as far west as Idaho and as far east as Pennsylvania drains through South Louisiana via the Mississippi and Atchafalaya Rivers, depositing silt in volumes that are sufficient, without intervention by mankind, to alter the landscape and the courses of rivers.

The Spanish laid the foundations of a colony but the Cajuns embraced the region as an Eden of sorts—a place where they could be left alone to

practice their religion and customs. They trapped the mammals and reptiles that were abundant along the bayous, eating the meat and selling the skins and pelts. They fished, raised cattle (Brahman and longhorn steers were reared in Louisiana well before they appeared in Texas), planted small crops and gathered the ubiquitous Spanish moss for its commercial value as stuffing in furniture and bedding.

To some extent, the Cajun ways have endured because of the relative isolation of Acadiana (since 1971 the official name for the region's 22 parishes). The isolation extended into this century. While the rest of the country was being stitched together by

the interstate highway system, Cajun Country was virtually untouched. Until the 1930's, there was no bridge over the Mississippi south of Vicksburg. Interstate 10 from Houston to New Orleans, by way of Lafayette and Baton Rouge, was not completed until 1973. Engineers simply had been stumped by the challenge of crossing the 18-mile-wide Atchafalaya River basin, North America's largest river-basin swamp.

Times have changed, but as recently as 1957 the *American Heritage Book of Great Historical Places* said this of the Cajuns: "Speaking an ancient French dialect, which few outsiders can follow, mixing little with the modern world, they earn a living by fishing, boating, trapping and by selling handwoven baskets and cloth. In a region of few roads, they live on simple wooden houseboats, dependent upon the waterways and the pirogue."

A drive from Houma, in the southeastern wetlands of Acadiana, to Eunice and Mamou, on the western plains, traverses the full range of Cajun life. The coastal marshlands, the swamps of the Mississippi Alluvial Plain and the moss-veiled waterways and forests of the Atchafalaya watershed are usually seen as the Cajun homeland. However, Cajun Country also embraces sugarcane fields and plantation mansions, wooded salt domes, cattle ranges on the western prairies and flooded rice paddies that produce, in the off-season, generous harvests of crawfish, the national food of Cajunland.

A FEAST FOR THE SENSES

Along the way, the senses are teased by the intriguing texture of life here. In spring, the fields flame with wildflowers and in autumn the skies are hazy with the drifting smoke of burning cane stubble. Roadside stands offer pecans, yams, and jellies and syrups made from the wild mayhaw berry. The rich aroma of freshly made boudin, a hot rice and pork sausage, and the spiced and fried pork rinds, called cracklins, rises from country stores. The wail of fiddles and accordions drifts from dance halls and saloons. The airwaves are filled with French-language radio broadcasts.

Although Cajun Country may be less isolated today, it is still uniquely Cajun. Exploring the narrow channels and maze of hushed, sunlit waterways by boat a few miles south of the bayou town of Houma, visitors see civilization materializing and vanishing in rapid succession. A cluster of middle-class homes, shaded by sprawling live oaks, has not yet passed from sight when the swamp claims the landscape. Ghostly veils of Spanish moss drip from towering cypress; alligators laze on the muddy banks; snowy egrets stand motionless in the

GOTHIC GRANDEUR
San Francisco, the most ornate home on the Great River Road, was built in 1854. Its extravagant and exuberant exterior cost its builder, Edmond Bozonier Marmillion, a fortune. In fact, the plantation's name is said to have evolved from the French slang sans frusquin, *meaning without a franc. The interior is famous for its Victorian furnishings, marbling and false woodgraining, and its huge wooden ceiling medallions.*

shallows and blue herons skim the inky water with six-foot wings.

Suddenly, the remnants of human presence reappear—a trapper's camp abandoned when the squatters were evicted by the landowners and, across a cove, a tiny cabin used by hunters during duck and deer seasons. Then, the primitive face of the land appears. A family of plump nutria, a South American rodent that grows as large as a beaver, huddles on a fallen willow branch; poisonous water snakes slither through a floating carpet of purple hyacinth and a bald eagle circles overhead.

Beyond the Gulf Intracoastal Waterway, where the vast, watery plain drops toward sea level, Annie Miller, a 78-year-old Cajun known widely as "Alligator Annie," cuts the outboard engine of her flatbottomed aluminum boat to just above idle and calls out in a voice that has pealed over these listless bayous for more than half a century: "Baaabies! Come, babies. Baaabies!"

Ten- and twelve-foot alligators, barely perceptible to the untrained eye, stir among the reeds and stumps of the riverbank, lifting their heads in recognition. Then they slink into the water and glide toward the boat and Annie's offering of raw chicken, their eyes protruding above the surface like dual periscopes. A few of Alligator Annie's passengers hoist cameras. Others stare entranced as the reptiles use their powerful tails to thrust nearly their full lengths out of the water and take the bait affixed to the end of a long pole.

This is the Cajun Country the world knows best, but in fact it is a remnant of a bygone era. Although some South Louisianians still harvest the swamps, living on houseboats and subsisting on nutria and muskrat pelts and reptile skins (25,000 alligators

are killed legally in the wild each year), they are a vanishing breed. "More Cajuns have pickup trucks than pirogues [the shallow boats propelled by poling]. The shantyboat is no longer first choice for economical housing and some of them live in real houses, on dry land, with paved sidewalks leading right down to paved roadways," notes the *Lafayette Daily Advertiser.*

Like Annie Miller, who now makes her living from tourists rather than trapping, most Cajuns work in an industry—oil and petrochemicals, shipping, commercial fishing, agriculture and tourism. The oil industry, in particular, brought high-paying jobs to the region, playing a big part in ending Cajun Country's rural isolation. However, the tradition-conscious Cajuns have managed to preserve the edifices and artifacts of their history.

THE TREE THAT IS A SHRINE

Saint Martinville was one of the first places in the region where the Cajuns settled. In Saint Martinville is the Evangeline Oak, immortalized by literature as much as by history. It was beside that stately live oak that Evangeline and her lover were briefly reunited, in Henry Wadsworth Longfellow's immortal poem of *Le Grand Dérangement, Evangeline.* Although the accuracy of the story is often questioned, the Evangeline Oak has become a shrine to the Cajun experience. Saint Martinville is also home to the restored St. Martin de Tours Catholic Church, established in 1765 and still the mother church of the Cajun people.

Throughout the region, magnificent manor houses from the plantation era have been restored for public viewing or as museums. At the Longfellow-Evangeline State Commemorative Area, just north of Saint Martinville, a typical raised 19th-century plantation house has been restored. The walls are made of a mixture of mud and moss (and sometimes deer hair), a material known locally as *bousillage.* In Thibodaux, an intact, self-contained plantation village consisting of 1840's-vintage houses, barns, slave cabins, schoolhouse, stables and general store endures as the Laurel Valley Village-Museum. In Jeanerette is a raised cottage that was floated up Bayou Teche after Cajuns settled there in 1790. New Iberia has the Church of the Epiphany, which was used as a hospital during the Civil War. Broussard House, moved from New Iberia to Vermilionville, an Acadian village in Lafayette, was built of pegged cypress logs—without any nails—in 1790 by Armand Broussard, the son of one of the very first Acadians to settle on the bayou.

The botanical splendor of the bayou area around New Iberia is displayed in several garden sanctu-

HALLOWEEN CAJUN-STYLE

Every Halloween, Shadows-on-the-Teche, an antebellum mansion overlooking Bayou Teche, celebrates in its own way. Candles, protected by paper bags, cast eerie shadows, and folk stories are recounted on the grounds, weather permitting.

aries: at Avery Island, Jungle Gardens is justly celebrated for its beautiful seasonal arrays of camellias, azaleas and tropical plants. Avery Island is not really an island, but rather a salt dome—salt-enriched rock forced upward by pressure from below to form a dome shape—one of many found in the Gulf states. This "island," encircled by a bayou, has been called a 2,500-acre "feast of the senses" because of its botanical riches, its refuge for cranes, egrets and herons, and for its cayenne pepper fields. It is no coincidence that New Iberia also produces that essential ingredient of Cajun cuisine, Tabasco hot pepper sauce.

Six miles away, another salt dome, Jefferson Island, has a 20-acre flower garden and the 1,300-acre Lake Peigneur, site of a strange industrial mishap that occurred in 1980. An oil exploration

CAJUN REVELRY
Clifton Chenier, left, was one of Zydeco's best-loved performers. The music, played on accordions and washboards with spoons, thimbles or bottle openers, was born in South Louisiana and the area has a number of annual Zydeco festivals. Cajun Country is known for its fairs and festivals, chief among them Mardi Gras. Lafayette's Mardi Gras, below, is the second-largest in the nation. There are seven parades during the four days preceding Ash Wednesday and they all feature floats, marching bands, dances and ongoing partying.

crew, working in the lake, drilled a hole into the dome below, where miners excavating salt had hollowed out chambers supported by salt pillars. The miners escaped, but the lake bed collapsed and nearly four billion gallons of water inundated the cavity, sucking barges, tugs and fishing boats down with it. The Delcambre Canal, which flows from the lake, was pulled backwards and eventually refilled the basin.

Just up the road from the bayous and swamps is the city of Lafayette, settled in the 1770's, and now home to more than 95,000 people. Lafayette attracted more Cajuns than any other settlement and today proudly calls itself the Capital of French Louisiana. Here, all the fragments of South Louisiana life converge. Despite its importance as a center for the local oil industry, Lafayette is still a small town at heart. Each September, the town hosts the *Festivals Acadiens*, a celebration of Cajun food, music and crafts. Lafayette is also the home of Acadian Village, a carefully recreated 19th-century Cajun village on a winding bayou. The site includes a number of simple cottages, a chapel and a general store. Most of the buildings are authentically furnished.

MAMOU'S SPECIAL MARDI GRAS

To the west and north of Lafayette is an area known as the Cajun Heartland. Here, the landscape changes from swamp to prairie and here the Acadians cling most stubbornly to tradition. Lafayette may be the Cajun capital, but at Mamou, roughly 40 miles to the northwest, Cajun tradition swings with abandon during Mardi Gras, the uproarious festival held on the last Tuesday before the start of Lent. In New Orleans, and even in Lafayette, Mardi Gras is a lavish festival marked by parades and balls. Mamou boasts that its Mardi Gras is the oldest, most traditional and the best organized of all. It is called the *Courir de Mardi Gras*—the Mardi Gras Run—and probably began in medieval Europe.

The *Courir de Mardi Gras* involves a troop of about 200 masked and costumed men who ride around the countryside, soliciting contributions of food from local farms. Everything they collect goes into a massive pot of gumbo cooked up and served by the women of the community at Mamou's American Legion Home. Copious amounts of food and drink are consumed, and an evening dance rounds out the celebrations, which end on the stroke of midnight and the arrival of Ash Wednesday.

Music, as much as language and geography, defines Cajun Country. In dozens of annual festivals, in night clubs and taverns, radio broadcasts and even at church socials, the music is celebrated with abandon.

As it has done for the past three decades, the door to Fred's Lounge in Mamou swings open early on Saturday morning and the austere, garage-size saloon begins to fill with beer drinkers, toe-tappers, musicians, spectators and technicians setting up for a live, four-hour broadcast on radio station KVPI in nearby Ville Platte. At nine o'clock sharp, a bowstring drags across a fiddle in a yelp reminiscent of a bagpipe. An accordion wheezes to life.

DOWNHOME COOKING
Louisiana crawfish are a regional specialty. In traditional dishes, these four-inch freshwater lobsters are boiled in their shells in a large pot with fresh corn, and flavored with spices. Hefty servings are heaped onto plates, and the crawfish are peeled by hand, and popped in the mouth.

Acoustic guitars and, occasionally, a pedal steel or triangle join the chase. The beat is a lively and energizing two-step, but the sound has overtones of a mournful wail—a genre born of exile and hardship underlaid with resolute joviality.

While outsiders refer to it as "Cajun" music, locals are more apt to call it "French," the language of the lyrics. Its base is western French and French-Acadian folk, but the influences that have shaped it are as varied as a pot of gumbo: Irish, Scottish, Anglo-American, Spanish. Germans contributed the accordion. Caribbean islanders of African descent swayed the beat with a hint of the blues and soul of Zydeco. Zydeco is South Louisiana's other unusual music species and the defining Zydeco instrument is a *frottoir*, a metal washboard played with thimbles, bottle openers or spoons.

Five hours after the broadcast at Fred's Lounge ends, another begins 10 miles away in Eunice, at the 70-year-old Liberty Theater, which was, in its previous incarnations, a movie house and a vaudeville stage. Each week, 600 to 700 locals and a few visitors line up for $2 tickets to *Rendez-Vous des Cajuns*, a live two-hour show, which features music, storytelling and downhome recipes. The broadcast is mostly in French, except for those English words and expressions—"pickup truck," "baseball cap," "moonshine"—for which there is no adequate French counterpart. An open area between the theater seats and the stage is used for dancing.

THE BOUNTY OF THE BAYOU

No matter what the occasion, Cajun Country's small-town restaurants and roadside diners are always waiting with what is the region's most treasured resource—its cuisine. Once considered impoverished, back-country cooking, Cajun delicacies have spread to upscale eateries in every corner of the country and Acadians consider their land the greatest natural pantry God has given anyone.

As applied to cuisine, the terms "Cajun" and "Creole" are often used interchangeably, but they are not the same, although the differences are sub-

PEPPER PICKER

On Avery Island, just south of New Iberia, the peppers that make Louisiana's famous Tabasco sauce are carefully handpicked. The spices and peppers used in the region's sauces have grown in the area around New Iberia since the late 18th century. One family, the McIlhennys, has manufactured Tabasco sauce at its Avery Island factory for four generations.

*Great flocks of egrets and herons
make Avery Island their home.
Here, in the morning fog,
an egret comes in for a landing
at a community nesting site.*

tle. Creole more aptly pertains to a New Orleans-style cuisine that has both French and Italian accents and relies more heavily on rich sauces.

Cajun food is hearty, country fare. Its staples are what the land has provided: crawfish, a freshwater crustacean that resembles a lobster; shrimp, which abounds in the Gulf of Mexico; rice and red beans; strawberries and yams; alligator and turtle; boudin and *andouille*, a lean, smoked pork sausage. Onion, garlic, tomatoes and cayenne pepper are typical seasonings in many local dishes.

A single dish can vary greatly according to available ingredients and the chef's mood. The most famous Cajun concoction is gumbo, a highly seasoned stew made with either seafood or meat and often thickened with filé powder—ground sassafras leaves. Jambalaya, another local specialty, can be made with beef, pork, sausage, chicken, seafood or any combination of those, stirred into a pot of rice, vegetables and seasonings.

FESTIVALS OF FOOD

The hearty cuisine of Cajun Country is exhibited at countless food festivals in South Louisiana each year. Cajuns have found dozens of ways to prepare crawfish, and the Breaux Bridge Crawfish Festival (held during early May in even-numbered years) shows them all off. At Gonzales—known since 1967 as the Jambalaya Capital of the World—the competition is fierce as cooks vie to produce the best jambalaya, which is then eaten by visitors to the International Jambalaya Championship (held in June). Bridge City is the scene of a gumbo festival in mid-October, while in late February the bayou

town of Broussard honors the humble boudin. Rice is a staple food of Cajun Country, and watery southern Louisiana is prime rice-growing country. To prove it, the town of Crowley, a few miles west of Lafayette, hosts an International Rice Festival each October.

While the face of Cajun country has changed in the last quarter of a century—man-made levees have tamed the fickle watershed and new highways have ended South Louisiana's splendid isolation—the devotion to Cajun culture probably ensures its survival. French, a tongue once forbidden on school grounds, has been reintroduced into classrooms. The Cajun fondness for wagering is manifest in

Cypress trees in the morning light and draped with Spanish moss lend an eerie aspect to the swamps and bayous of Cajun Country. Perfectly suited to the watery habitat is the Alligator mississippiensis. The 12-foot-long specimen seen below is resting on a sand bar, but the leathery creatures are not always so placid. They can move on land or in the water with amazing speed.

race tracks, legal cockfighting pits and card bars. And the legendary Cajun humor has probably been finely honed, rather than blunted, by the influx of outsiders.

A visitor, befuddled by maps and road signs, stops at a small gas station in the outskirts of what appears to be a small town and asks the proprietor, "How far is it to Eunice?"

"Wall, mah fran," the man behind the counter drawls in Cajun English, "Da-pen hah you go. Go up tru Mamou, be 'bot 20 mile. Go rown tru Basile, be 'bot 18 mile or some. But stay rat wear you are, you dair."

Son-of-a-gun, we'll have big fun on the bayou.

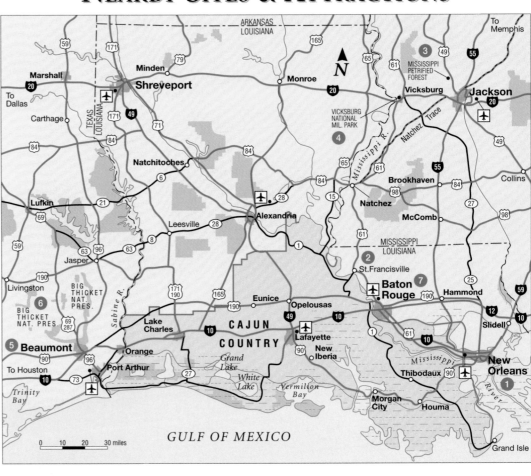

Morning fog envelops Jackson Square in the heart of the French Quarter of New Orleans. The spire of St. Louis Cathedral is barely visible.

① NEW ORLEANS

The 75-block French Quarter of New Orleans—laid out in a grid pattern in 1721— contains historic buildings, museums, antique shops, art galleries and Bourbon Street jazz clubs. Some of the district's period houses can be visited, including the 1826 Beauregard-Keyes House, which boasts a 25-by-50-foot ballroom. St. Louis Cathedral, whose central spire is higher than any other building in the French Quarter, borders Jackson Square—the heart of the district. Uptown is the Garden District, an area of elegant Greek Revival antebellum mansions and lavish gardens settled by Americans of Anglo-Saxon origin who immigrated south after the Louisiana Purchase brought the area under the U.S. flag. The St. Charles Avenue Streetcar, America's oldest continuously operating street railway, connects the Garden District to the French Quarter. The Mardi Gras parade begins two weeks before Mardi Gras Day—Shrove Tuesday. Located on Hwys. 10, 59 and 55.

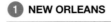

② ST. FRANCISVILLE

St. Francisville was built along a narrow ridge that local lore describes as being "two miles wide and two yards long." The area's planters made history in 1810 when they revolted against Spanish claims by forming a republic that flew a lone star flag for 76 days. Rosedown, one of Louisiana's most dazzling pre-Civil War plantations, is located in St. Francisville and is furnished with antiques. It is surrounded by 30 acres of formal gardens that include 100-year-old camellias and azaleas. In 1819, the Barrows of North Carolina built Afton Villa, a Gothic Revival mansion. Although the home burned to the ground in 1963, its ruins are surrounded by a spectacular seasonal garden and park. Located 30 miles northwest of Baton Rouge near the junction of Hwys. 10 and 61.

The modest wooden front porch of Rosedown Plantation in St. Francisville is part of the small main house. Two monumental wings were added in 1858.

③ MISSISSIPPI PETRIFIED FOREST

Thousands of years of erosion have exposed giant petrified sequoia, fir, maple and spurge logs here, some of which are 36 million years old. The trees were carried to this area by a prehistoric river. Stripped of limbs, bark and roots by the journey and buried in sand and silt, the logs slowly absorbed mineral-rich silica and eventually turned to stone. This fossilized log forest is the only one of its kind east of the Mississippi. A nature trail winds through a section of the park that has been dubbed the miniature Badlands because of its eroded pink and red cliffs. Another part of the trail leads through a forest of pine, elm, oak and plum trees. A museum at the visitor center is devoted to petrified wood, gems, minerals and fossils. Located 13 miles north of Jackson off Hwy. 49.

④ VICKSBURG

Vicksburg's strategic location on 200-foot bluffs overlooking the Mississippi River made it a vital Confederate stronghold during the Civil War. After two attacks and a 47-day siege in which many townspeople almost starved to death, Vicksburg surrendered to General Ulysses S. Grant on July 4, 1863. The siege is often reenacted in July at the Vicksburg National Military Park, the site of Union siege lines. Shirley House, once Confederate head-quarters, is the only building in the park from the Civil War. The remains of the *USS Cairo*, a restored Union gunboat raised from the bottom of the Mississippi River 100 years after it was sunk by Confederate troops, is also on display. The Old Court House Museum, a Greek Revival building, houses period furniture and furnishings that once graced the city's antebellum mansions. Located on Hwys. 80 and 61.

⑤ BEAUMONT

Beaumont became famous at the turn of the century when oil gushed 200 feet into the air at Spindletop Hill, Texas's first major oil field. The population of the town grew from 9,000 to 50,000 in six months as major oil companies moved in to take advantage of the liquid gold. By 1901 there were 285 operating oil wells at Spindletop Hill. Beaumont was also assured its starring role in the petroleum industry when it became an important port after the Neches River was deepened for shipping in 1908. Visitors can relive the excitement of the town's heyday at Gladys City Boomtown, a reconstruction of the rough clap-board houses, surveyor's office, saloon and pharma-cy, all of which are furnished with period antiques and artifacts. The Texas Energy Museum profiles a day on the oil field and contains a 120-foot-long wall of history highlighting the development of energy resources from the 18th century until the present. Located on the Neches River on Hwys. 10 and 96.

⑥ BIG THICKET NATIONAL PRESERVE

Established to protect the "biological crossroads of North America," Big Thicket National Preserve was designated an International Biosphere Reserve by

A 200-year-old alley of moss-draped oaks leads to the plantation house of Afton Villa, located four miles outside of St. Francisville.

the United Nations in 1981. The 84,550 acres of the preserve contain pine and hardwood forests, bayou, swamplands, grasslands, meadows and desert that support an incredible variety of flora and fauna. Called "an American ark," the preserve is home to a great diversity of wildlife, including almost 300 different bird species, armadillos and bobcats. Nearly 1,000 flowering plants, including 20 orchid types, grow here. The preserve may be accessed by car on local roads. Located off Hwy. 69.

⑦ BATON ROUGE

Baton Rouge, the capital city of Louisiana, was named by its French founders for a red post that marked the boundary between two Indian tribes. Now a major Mississippi River port, Baton Rouge is a city of restored antebellum mansions and is one of the best places to sample Cajun and Creole cuisine. The art-deco Louisiana State Capitol building (Huey P. Long was assassinated here) is 34 stories high, the tallest state house in the nation. It contains displays of Louisiana folklife and has an observation tower with a commanding view of the Mississippi. Magnolia Mound is one of the oldest plantations in the state and has been restored to reflect the lifestyle of the early 1800's. Baton Rouge visitors can also tour the *USS Kidd*, a World War II destroyer; a neighboring museum contains model ships, maritime artifacts and a restored P-40 Flying Tiger fighter plane. Located at the intersection of Hwys. 10 and 12.

The crenellated Gothic-style Old State Capitol in Baton Rouge was built in 1849 and overlooks the Mississippi River. It is now the Louisiana Center of Political and Governmental History, known especially for its spiral staircase and stained-glass dome.

TEXAS HILL COUNTRY

*Probably the most famous place
in the Texas Hill Country
is practically no place at all.*

It is one edifice of commerce—a combination post office, general store, dance hall, saloon, domino parlor and all-around idling ground—beside an ancient live oak tree and a few scattered, weather-beaten domiciles. Depending on who's stretching the truth, you may be told that the population is 20 or maybe 25, and if you don't know where it is, you'll have trouble knowing when you are there.

Though little more than a pebble on the gentle rises formed by primordial limestone and granite upheavals, the tiny hamlet of Luckenbach intruded into the national consciousness in the late 1970's on the crest of a pop culture craze known as Texas Chic. That was the Age of the Urban Cowboy, when exotic-skin boots, faded jeans, Stetsons and belt buckles broader than flour tortillas broke across the state line and infected fashion slaves from Milwaukee to Pittsburgh.

Country music was the elemental medium of the movement's tailor-made, cavalier mythology. Nearby Austin, sometimes recognized as the state capital but better known then as the place where Willie Nelson hung out, was reputed to be the

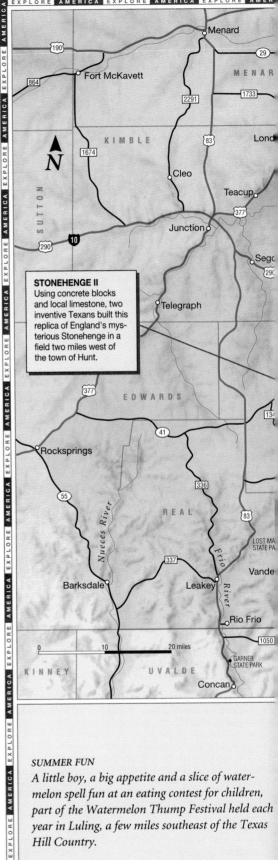

RAMSHACKLE RELIC

The weather-beaten general store in Luckenbach serves as post office, dance hall, saloon and blacksmith's shop. Settled in the 1850's by German pioneers, the tiny hamlet was rediscovered in the 1970's; townsfolk had to stop putting up city limit signs because souvenir hunters stole them as fast as they were posted. The town is privately owned and the general store is still open for business.

OVER THE HILL

Overleaf: Fields of wildflowers brighten the hills in spring. The scenery changes with the seasons and with each curve of the back roads. Named for its rolling terrain, the Texas Hill Country was formed as a result of the uplift which created the Balcones Escarpment.

most "laid back" big city in America—until a troubadour named Waylon Jennings sang of a yearning that was the core of the craze: To escape the coat-and-tie, diamond ring, four-car garage high society, drop out and "get back to the basics."

"Out in Luckenbach, Texas," he sang, "ain't nobody feelin' no pain." Like the faithful on a pilgrimage, followers trouped to the town made famous by a song. Hondo Crouch, a grizzled humorist and sly promoter who happened to own Luckenbach, tried to make it what everyone expected—a Texas Chic theme park of Saturday night two-stepping, longneck beer, chili cookoffs and homespun homilies. "Everybody's somebody in Luckenbach," says a sign on the saloon wall.

Hondo died, and so eventually did Texas Chic. But the town of Luckenbach lives on not only as a tourist haunt but as an icon—the hard kernel that defines the soul and heartbeat of an area with soft, arguable boundaries.

HILLS MEET THE HIGH PLAINS

Situated in the heart of Texas, the Hill Country is a 90-by-115-mile ellipse. It stretches from Austin west to Llano and Junction, where the hills meet the high plains; loops south through Telegraph, Rocksprings and Barksdale, and back eastward, across the upper edge of Uvalde and Medina Counties, where the Balcones Escarpment tumbles down from the Edwards Plateau toward the Rio Grande Valley. San Antonio, a popular starting point for the Hill Country, is at the southeast edge of the oval's boundary, but just outside of it.

STONEHENGE II
Using concrete blocks and local limestone, two inventive Texans built this replica of England's mysterious Stonehenge in a field two miles west of the town of Hunt.

SUMMER FUN

A little boy, a big appetite and a slice of watermelon spell fun at an eating contest for children, part of the Watermelon Thump Festival held each year in Luling, a few miles southeast of the Texas Hill Country.

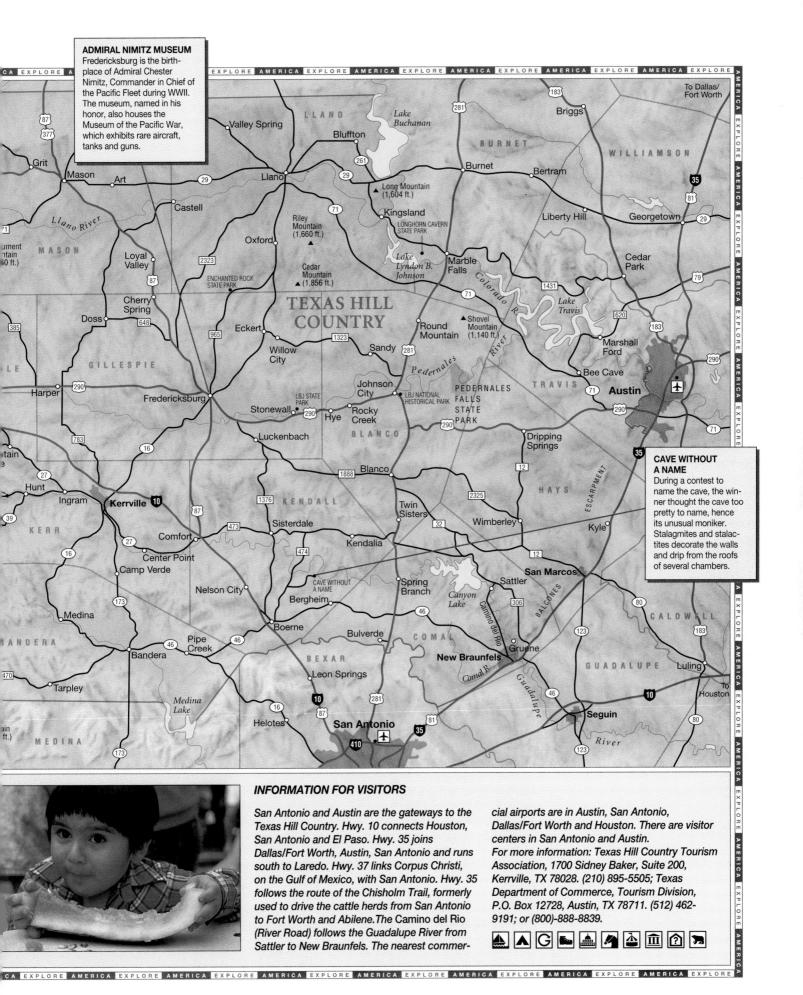

ADMIRAL NIMITZ MUSEUM
Fredericksburg is the birth-place of Admiral Chester Nimitz, Commander in Chief of the Pacific Fleet during WWII. The museum, named in his honor, also houses the Museum of the Pacific War, which exhibits rare aircraft, tanks and guns.

CAVE WITHOUT A NAME
During a contest to name the cave, the winner thought the cave too pretty to name, hence its unusual moniker. Stalagmites and stalactites decorate the walls and drip from the roofs of several chambers.

INFORMATION FOR VISITORS

San Antonio and Austin are the gateways to the Texas Hill Country. Hwy. 10 connects Houston, San Antonio and El Paso. Hwy. 35 joins Dallas/Fort Worth, Austin, San Antonio and runs south to Laredo. Hwy. 37 links Corpus Christi, on the Gulf of Mexico, with San Antonio. Hwy. 35 follows the route of the Chisholm Trail, formerly used to drive the cattle herds from San Antonio to Fort Worth and Abilene. The Camino del Rio (River Road) follows the Guadalupe River from Sattler to New Braunfels. The nearest commercial airports are in Austin, San Antonio, Dallas/Fort Worth and Houston. There are visitor centers in San Antonio and Austin.
For more information: Texas Hill Country Tourism Association, 1700 Sidney Baker, Suite 200, Kerrville, TX 78028. (210) 895-5505; Texas Department of Commerce, Tourism Division, P.O. Box 12728, Austin, TX 78711. (512) 462-9191; or (800)-888-8839.

NOCTURNAL CREATURES

Bobcats and armadillos are just some of the animals that live in and around the Lost Maples State Natural Area. Both these animals are secretive and elusive, and are only active at night. Although the bobcat is North America's most common wildcat, it is rarely spotted. The armadillo's armor protects its back and sides from attacks by predators.

It is a region of sparse population, abundant wildlife, curious geological formations, rugged beauty and a history dense with cultural diversity. The late president Lyndon B. Johnson was the most renowned native of the hills (the LBJ State Park on the Pedernales River near the town of Stonewall is named for him) and his description of the country bears witness to his love for it: "There is no other place that can do for me what this land and what this water and what these people and what these hills and these surroundings can do. It is a harsh, unyielding land that does not easily give of life. Even the huge live oaks are gnarled and twisted as if to show that their existence was not won without a struggle....But it is also a bold and beautiful land, where the air is clear and the water is pure and the wildflowers, flashing in the sun, can make you catch your breath with their beauty—where the deer will come sniffing up to your back door while a meal is cooking."

Until a billion years ago, this part of Texas was a shallow ocean basin 150 miles off the coast of North America. A continental collision thrust the sea floor upwards, creating in the process an enormous subterranean smelter that melted rocks and layers of limestone into mounds of granite now known as the Llano Uplift or the Central Mineral Region of the Texas Hill Country.

The most visible remnant of that occurrence is at Enchanted Rock State Park, located southwest of Llano, where a 75-acre dome of pink granite—the second-largest such deposit in the United States—rises 325 feet above an adjacent creek bed. The granite is approximately one billion years old and ranks among the oldest exposed rock in North America. The name for the area derived from an Indian belief that the rock was haunted or enchanted because it emitted eerie moaning noises as the granite expanded and contracted with changing temperatures. More recently, the wailing stone has been a siren call to New Agers who believe it possesses mystic powers.

The geology has given the park an odd texture of plant and animal life. Persimmon, mesquite, Mexican buckeye and prickly-pear cactus typical of the arid Trans-Pecos prosper alongside the elm, pecan and oak varieties common to the lush forests of East Texas. A tropical fern called *Blechnum occidentale* is found nowhere in the United States except at Enchanted Rock State Park and in a few remote areas of Florida. More than 150 species of birds reside in or visit the park regularly, sharing it with white-tailed deer, fox squirrels, armadillos, rabbits and lizards.

Other anomalies of nature abound. Along the canyons in the Frio River watershed between Leakey and Concan, scattered "islands" of vegetation thrive hundreds of miles from their usual environment. Near Vanderpool, the canyon is home to the "lost maples," so called because they are remnants of the Pleistocene Ice Age. The canyon has given them refuge from the arid winds and warm temperature that otherwise would have eradicated them. Other varieties—American smoketree and Canadian moonseed, most notably—have shared the canyon haven, far from others of their kind.

Among Texans, the Hill Country is one of the most beloved regions of the state, a place in the mind as much as the atlas. It is coveted for its deep blue lakes and fast-running rivers, for its fields of bluebonnets in the spring and canyons splashed with turning maple leaves in autumn, for its apple orchards, vineyards, dude ranches, historic architecture, rustic inns, mellow days and starlit nights.

The small towns are timeless and close-knit, reveling in simple pleasures and easy rhythms. At Christmastime, the residents of tiny Johnson City—named for the pioneering ancestors of former president Lyndon Baines Johnson—adorn their courthouse, homes, businesses and churches with 350,000 lights. Kerrville, reputed to have one of the healthiest climates in the nation, hosts an annual Texas Heritage Music Festival that includes a tribute to Jimmie Rodgers; and the pride of Burnet is the Hill Country Flyer, a steam locomotive with 4 coaches and 33 miles of track.

Although the hills were occupied first by Indians and then Spanish soldiers trying to conquer what was then a part of Mexico, the most prominent ethnic imprint on the region is European. In the mid-1840's, the Republic of Texas granted to the German Emigration Society 3,800,000 acres between the Llano and Pecos Rivers.

Fredericksburg, in the Pedernales River valley, became a way-station for German settlers who came from Gulf Coast ports by foot and ox cart. Many of the limestone houses and public buildings they erected are still standing. Other traces of their culture and language have likewise endured. "Historische Bezirks Tour, Friedrichsburg, Gegrundet 1846," says the cover of a brochure listing local points of interest. The Priess Building, Wahrmund Home, Felix van der Stucken House, the Vereins Kirche (Society's Church)—all are evidence of the pervasive German legacy. An architectural oddity of the town is its Sunday Houses. These miniature wood and stone dwellings were used by farmers on weekends when they would come into town to pick up supplies, visit friends, and attend church service on Sunday.

FRONTIER FARMERS
Pioneering life of the early 1900's is carried out by costumed interpreters at the Sauer-Beckmann Farmstead, located within the LBJ State Park, east of Stonewall. The midwife who delivered former president Lyndon B. Johnson grew up in the limestone house, above. There is also a one-room log cabin, and a wood frame house, both built around the turn of the century.

Erosion has exposed the massive dome of pink granite rock at the Enchanted Rock State Park. Located in the heart of the Texas Hill Country, the 1,643-acre park provides opportunities for rock climbers, hikers and rockhounds.

CULTURAL COWBOYS

Even in Bandera, with its Hispanic name and old west ambience (the town calls itself the Cowboy Capital of the World and stages rodeos three times a week throughout the summer), the influence of East European settlers still lingers. The main drag looks vaguely like a turn-of-the-century cowtown, and cattle ranches snuggle up to the city limits, but the tribal history of Bandera is better written in the cemetery beside St. Stanislaus Catholic Church. It is the second-oldest Polish church in the U.S. The headstones there are etched in Polish: Mazurek...Adamietz...Jureczki...Pyka...Kalka.

New Braunfels, on the southeastern fringe of the hills between Austin and San Antonio, was founded by Prince Carl of Solms-Braunfels—and, like Fredericksburg, embraces its Germanic heritage devoutly. Its sausage houses and bakeries dish up authentic fare and in its *biergarten* polka bands ruffle the placid evenings along the spring-fed Comal River, which begins and ends inside the township. Each year, New Braunfels' 10-day Wurstfest, one of the largest celebrations of German culture in the United States, draws 125,000 visitors who come for the oompah bands, parades and parties, and sausages of every description.

Moreover, New Braunfels is located on the banks of the Guadalupe River, one of the premier recreation waterways not just of the Texas Hill Country but of the entire state. Every year, approximately 350,000 adventurers, most bearing rubber inner tubes, arrive at its banks to float the 17 miles of chill, rapid waters between Canyon Lake and New Braunfels.

Along the way, the Guadalupe passes the little settlement of Gruene, pronounced "Green," a once-thriving farm community that became virtually a ghost town following the Great Depression. In the mid-1970's, a group of investors purchased the land and buildings and turned them into a resort of pure Texana. Both the dance hall and general mercantile store were reopened. The gristmill was turned into a restaurant. The winery was reactivated. The meandering, *fachwerk* mansion, originally built by Ernst Gruene, was converted to a bed-and-breakfast inn. Gruene is what Luckenbach might have become if folks hadn't kept stealing the city limit signs.

Three anglers try their luck by a waterfall on Lake Buchanan—the highest and widest lake in the Highland Lake chain. The chain was created by the Buchanan Dam, one of the largest multi-arch dams in the world.

PRICKLY TREASURES

The brightly colored flowers of pincushion cacti add a splash of color to the arid prairie land of the Texas Hill Country. The cactus is native to the western United States, Mexico and Cuba.

"Many a Texan's dream is to retire with a little rancho (in the Hill Country)," wrote Joe Cummings in the *Texas Handbook*. In 1981, a petroleum geologist named Baxter Adams did just that, but instead of retiring, he brought apple growing to Medina, which was on the way to becoming a ghost town. Adams ignored the scoffs of agronomists, who said the fruit could not prosper.

There is very little agriculture in the Hill Country. Millennia of erosion have carved out spectacular valleys and canyons, but left the soil shallow and inhospitable to any but the least demanding of crops. Baxter Adams was told that apples were unsuitable for the bottom land he had chosen along Love Creek. Just 10 years later, dozens of other planters, encouraged by Baxter's success, had joined him and their orchards were producing 50,000 bushels of apples from dwarf trees each year. Medina soon boasted a full-blown apple festival.

It was another example of the permutations of nature that give the Hill Country a special life, as capable of renewal as the ghost towns that occasionally return from the dead. But it is its timeless nature that gives the region its allure and mystique.

In *A President's Country*, Texas geologist Peter Flawn said, "It is an old and stable land which has withstood well the vicissitudes of time. It is very much likely to be the same a hundred or a thousand years in the future."

One imagines that in that distant time it will still be true that in Luckenbach, Texas, there ain't nobody feelin' no pain.

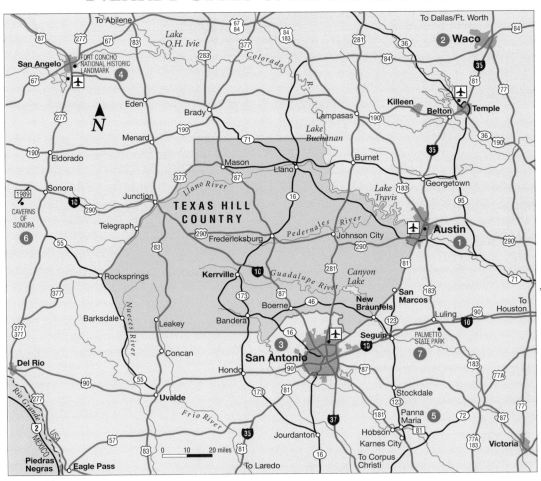

This butterfly-shaped calcite formation is one of the most unusual and beautiful helictites in the Caverns of Sonora.

① AUSTIN

The capital of Texas was named after Stephen F. Austin, who brought the first American settlers to the then Spanish-ruled territory. The city boasts an impressive variety of museums, historic sites and recreational areas. The imposing domed State Capitol building is one of Austin's most famous landmarks. Built of Texas pink granite, it is actually seven feet higher than the Capitol in Washington, D.C. Austin's oldest building is the French Legation, built in 1840 by Comte Alphonse Dubois de Saligny, France's representative to the independent Republic of Texas. Other sites include the Lyndon B. Johnson Library and Museum and the house occupied by William Sydney Porter, better known as O. Henry. The noted short story writer lived in Austin from 1882 until 1898. He left after facing bank embezzlement charges and serving a three-and-a-half-year jail term. Just east of the city lies the National Wildflower Research Center, which promotes the study and propagation of native plants. Located on Hwy. 35 between San Antonio and Waco.

② WACO

Located on the Brazos River, Waco was for many years an important stop on the Chisholm Trail, the cattle trail that led north from San Antonio to Fort Worth and Abilene, Kansas. John A. Roebling, designer of the Brooklyn Bridge, consulted on Waco's famous Suspension Bridge, the first bridge to span Texas's longest river. The 475-foot structure was built in 1869-70, and was for some years the nation's largest bridge. A century later it became a pedestrian crossing. Waco got its start as Fort Fisher, a Texas Ranger outpost established in 1837. At the Texas Ranger Hall of Fame, a replica fort and a museum immortalize the exploits of these renowned lawmen. Waco is also famous as the birthplace of Dr. Pepper, the soft drink formulated in 1885 by local pharmacist R.S. Lazenby. A recreated soda fountain and museum are housed in the company's original 1906 bottling plant, which is listed in the National Register of Historic Places. Located on Hwy. 35 between Austin and Dallas.

③ SAN ANTONIO

This beautiful old city on the banks of the San Antonio River was the capital of Texas during the days of Spanish rule. It was near the banks of the river in 1718 that the Spanish founded the Mission San Antonio de Valero (known as the Alamo), the first and most famous of the city's five Franciscan missions. The Alamo was the scene of the epic siege of 1836, in which 189 Texan patriots died fighting for Texan independence. The other four missions make up San Antonio Missions National Historical Park. Today, the Paseo del Rio (River Walk), a beautifully landscaped pedestrian promenade shaded by cypress trees, meanders through the city center along both sides of the river just below street level. Vestiges of Spanish influence are seen at the Spanish Governor's Palace, an adobe-walled structure built from 1722 to 1749; and at La Villita, a collection of 27 reconstructed adobe houses on the site of San Antonio's earliest residential district. Located south of Austin on Hwys. 10, 35 and 37.

4 FORT CONCHO NATIONAL HISTORIC LANDMARK, SAN ANGELO

Sixteen original buildings still stand on this 40-acre National Historic Landmark, one of the best preserved and most beautiful frontier posts in Texas. Fort Concho, established in 1867 to protect settlers and stagecoach traffic, was decommissioned in 1889 after the frontier moved westward. During the 1870's, German craftsmen from Fredericksburg were employed to construct the limestone barrack buildings, which have rafters made from pecan wood. Five of the original 23 buildings have been reconstructed. In Barracks V, costumed interpreters reenact the daily routines of enlisted men of the time. Located on East Avenue D in downtown San Angelo, south of Abilene.

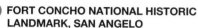

5 PANNA MARIA

Founded by settlers from Upper Silesia in 1854, this little town is reputed to be the oldest Polish settlement in the U.S. Older members of the community still speak a Silesian dialect. The town was named for the Virgin Mary in gratitude for the settlers' safe arrival after a difficult overland journey from their landing place at Galveston. Panna Maria's Immaculate Conception Church dates from 1877, and the town contains a number of stone cottages from the original settlement. Located southeast of San Antonio off Hwy. 123.

6 CAVERNS OF SONORA

Spectacular multicolored stalactites, stalagmites, helictites and crystal formations, some resembling marine corals, decorate the walls of these limestone caverns. One of the most beautiful formations is a helictite known as "The Butterfly" because of its roughly symmetrical, translucent "wings." This drapery formation is the only known example of its type in the world. Guided cave tours take visitors through one-and-a-half miles of chambers and passages. Located about 8 miles west of Sonora on Ranch Road 1989 (exit 292 off Hwy. 10).

7 PALMETTO STATE PARK

This 268-acre preserve, located on the San Marcos River, boasts 550 species of eastern and western plants, including dwarf palmetto. Its unusual mix of natural environments combines hardwood forests of pecan, elm and oak with the stands of cactus typical of the Southwest. Until the 1970's the park boasted naturally occurring artesian and warm springs, reputed to be curative, mud boils and peat deposits. Oil and gas drilling has upset the water table, however, and only warm artesian wells remain. This is a popular destination for birdwatchers, particularly in winter. Located 7 miles south of Luling on Hwy. 183.

San Antonio's River Walk, left, draws visitors and residents to its cafes, boutiques and restaurants night and day. Riverboat tours and strolling mariachi bands add to the atmosphere. Above are the remains of the 18th-century Mission San José, one of the five original missions in San Antonio, the most famous of which is the Alamo.

SAN JUAN SOJOURN

Reminiscent of the Swiss Alps, southwest Colorado's mountains offer heart-stopping scenery.

Spring comes to the San Juan Mountains in June. The 25-foot snowpack starts to melt, feeding boisterous streams that come roaring down from the high country. As they gather force, the streams give birth to some of the Southwest's biggest rivers: the Rio Grande, San Juan, Dolores, San Miguel, Animas and Uncompahgre. The names of the rivers and the mountains them-selves speak of the region's Native American and European heritage. The Spaniards christened the mountains in honor of Saint John; the Utes looked to them as the source of visions and as hunting grounds.

In summer, greens of many hues soften the rugged profile of the San Juans: lime-green aspens in new leaf, deep green spruce and fir and the short-lived gray-green tundra plants. The alpine meadows are alight with paintbrush, lupine, columbine and bistort. Herds of elk return to graze on their summer ranges.

After the brief but busy tourist season, summer draws to a close in August. Usually by November

EXPLORE AMERICA EXPLORE AMERICA EXPLORE AM

HIKER'S HEAVEN

With Lizard Head Peak rising in the background, a solitary hiker takes in the grandeur of a small slice of the Uncompahgre National Forest. Uncompahgre is a Ute word meaning "rocks that make red water."

THE LIZARD HEAD
Created by volcanic action, the Lizard Head is a 400-foot-high sheer rock tower.

the snow has again returned to the high country. And by November the black rivers are lined with ice, and naked aspens form soft gray clumps amidst the dark spruces. An ermine, in a perfect white winter coat, dives into snowbanks.

Winters are often long and cold. Three hundred inches of snowfall is common at the highest elevations of the San Juans. The mountains cast long shadows in mid-afternoon; on some days the small towns tucked against the peaks—Telluride, Ouray, Rico, Silverton and Lake City—feel like iceboxes. While locals often fly south for the season, visitors, some of them from southern climes, flock in for a week, staying where they can walk out their front doors and hit the ski slopes.

But after the aspen leaves have fallen, and before the snow is too deep, the San Juans are silent. All the campgrounds are empty; many windows are boarded shut. You can walk down the middle of a street and nothing much but a few barking dogs will denote your presence. The merchants in the several shops that remain open now have the time to talk to visitors.

The San Juans are a kingdom of 10,000 to 12,000 square miles of mountains in southwest Colorado. Actually a complex group of ranges, they include among others the Needle and Rico mountains and the Sneffels and Grenadier ranges. All are young mountains, rough and steep, with knife-edged peaks and ridges that look like pillars holding up the crystal blue sky.

THE HIGH LANDS

Overleaf: The San Juan Mountains rise behind the almost-neon glow of aspen near Telluride. The town was named for tellurium, an element found with the gold and silver that was once mined here.

INFORMATION FOR VISITORS

From Denver, take Hwy. 70 to Grand Junction, and then go south on Hwy. 50 and Hwy. 550; from Albuquerque, take Hwy. 25 north to Santa Fe, and Hwy. 84 to Pagosa Springs. For brochures and information on the spot, there is a Welcome Center on Hwy. 160 at Cortez. Airports are located at Montrose, Telluride, Grand Junction, Cortez and Durango. The San Juan

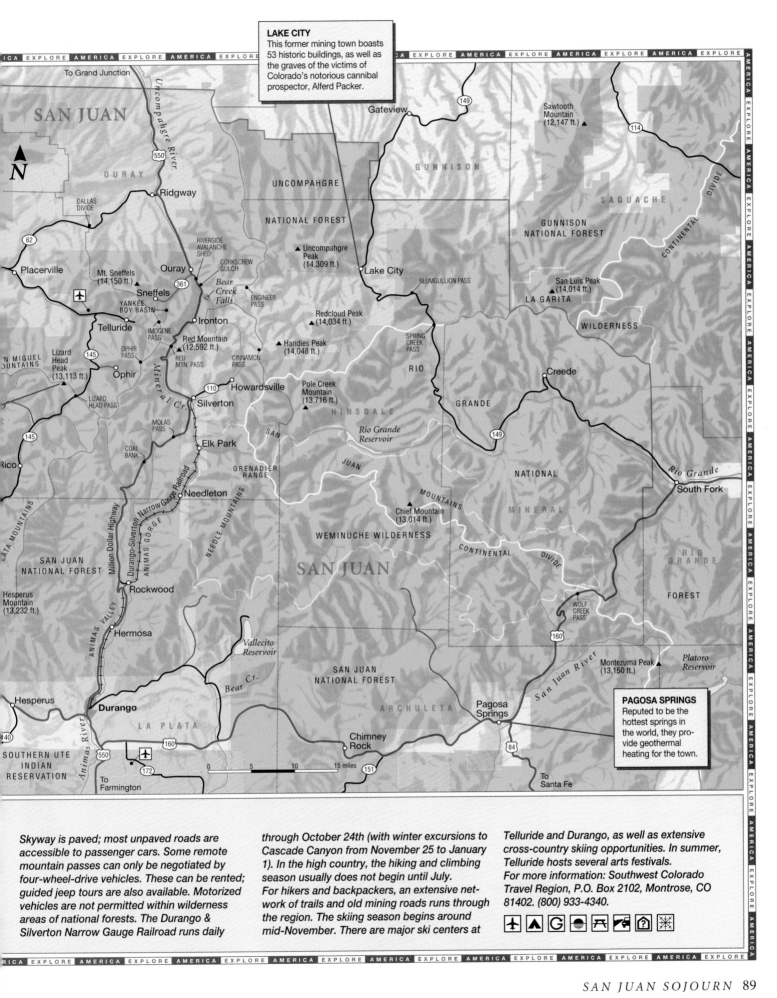

LAKE CITY
This former mining town boasts 53 historic buildings, as well as the graves of the victims of Colorado's notorious cannibal prospector, Alferd Packer.

PAGOSA SPRINGS
Reputed to be the hottest springs in the world, they provide geothermal heating for the town.

To Grand Junction

SAN JUAN

OURAY

Uncompahgre River

Ridgway

DALLAS
DIVIDE

UNCOMPAHGRE

NATIONAL FOREST

GUNNISON

Gateview

Sawtooth
Mountain
(12,147 ft.) ▲

SAGUACHE

CONTINENTAL DIVIDE

GUNNISON
NATIONAL FOREST

RIVERSIDE
AVALANCHE
SHED

Placerville

Mt. Sneffels
(14,150 ft.) ▲

CORKSCREW
GULCH

Ouray

Uncompahgre
Peak
(14,309 ft.) ▲

Lake City

SLUMGULLION PASS

San Luis Peak
▲ (14,014 ft.)

LA GARITA

Sneffels

YANKEE
BOY BASIN

Bear
Creek
Falls

ENGINEER
PASS

WILDERNESS

Telluride

Ironton

IMOGENE
PASS

Red Mountain
(12,592 ft.) ▲

Redcloud Peak
▲ (14,034 ft.)

SPRING
CREEK
PASS

Creede

Lizard
Head
Peak
(13,113 ft.)

OPHIR
PASS

RED
MTN. PASS

CINNAMON
PASS

Handies Peak
(14,048 ft.) ▲

RIO

LIZARD
HEAD PASS

Ophir

Mineral Cr.

Howardsville

Silverton

Pole Creek
Mountain
(13,716 ft.) ▲

HINSDALE

GRANDE

Rio Grande
Reservoir

149

Rio Grande

South Fork

MOLAS
PASS

Elk Park

COAL
BANK

SAN

JUAN

NATIONAL

MINERAL

Rico

GRENADIER
RANGE

Needleton

MOUNTAINS

Chief Mountain
(13,014 ft.) ▲

RIO
GRANDE

SAN JUAN
NATIONAL FOREST

Hesperus
Mountain
(13,232 ft.)

Rockwood

WEMINUCHE WILDERNESS

SAN JUAN

CONTINENTAL DIVIDE

FOREST

Hermosa

WOLF
CREEK
PASS

Vallecito
Reservoir

160

Montezuma Peak
(13,150 ft.) ▲

Platoro
Reservoir

Hesperus

Durango

LA PLATA

Bear Cr.

SAN JUAN
NATIONAL FOREST

Pagosa
Springs

San Juan River

SOUTHERN UTE
INDIAN
RESERVATION

Chimney
Rock

84

0   5   10   15 miles

151

To
Farmington

To
Santa Fe

SAN JUAN SOJOURN 89

Skyway is paved; most unpaved roads are accessible to passenger cars. Some remote mountain passes can only be negotiated by four-wheel-drive vehicles. These can be rented; guided jeep tours are also available. Motorized vehicles are not permitted within wilderness areas of national forests. The Durango & Silverton Narrow Gauge Railroad runs daily through October 24th (with winter excursions to Cascade Canyon from November 25 to January 1). In the high country, the hiking and climbing season usually does not begin until July.

For hikers and backpackers, an extensive network of trails and old mining roads runs through the region. The skiing season begins around mid-November. There are major ski centers at Telluride and Durango, as well as extensive cross-country skiing opportunities. In summer, Telluride hosts several arts festivals.

For more information: Southwest Colorado Travel Region, P.O. Box 2102, Montrose, CO 81402. (800) 933-4340.

The highest peak in the San Juans is Uncompahgre, 14,309 feet above sea level. Joining it are another dozen "fourteeners," their summits the sought-after goals of the mountain-climbing set. Radiating in all directions from these dizzying peaks are narrow, dark canyons with names like Corkscrew Gulch. Along highways, or more adventurous four-wheel-drive roads, many passes—Ophir, Engineer, Imogene, Lizard Head, Red Mountain, Slumgullion and Wolf Creek—take you above 10,000 feet. Their crossings are always momentous. The Continental Divide marks the crest of the San Juans. In this region it makes a big westerly meander before shooting back to cross into New Mexico.

The San Juans are forceful, wild, inspiring mountains, rising a mile above the valleys, which are already at 8,000 and 9,000 feet. These mountains can at times be formidable and unapproachable. They always strike wonder—when a full moon shines on their snowy countenance or the early morning sun suffuses them in soft peach light. As one writer has said: "Spirit, not height, is the true measure of mountains." The San Juans have an undeniable spirit.

The rock record revealed in these mountains is more complete than even that of the Grand Canyon. Ancient, hard quartzite and gneiss close to two billion years old form the soul of the San Juans. In some places, gigantic ripple marks are preserved in them, created by water lapping over mud more

OURAY'S CHARMS

The Victorian homes of Ouray, right, at times seem incongruous in the rough mountain setting. The town started in 1876 with a silver strike, but by the turn of the century was mining gold. It has been designated a historic district. The Ouray Hot Springs Pool and Park, above, is listed on the National Register of Historic Places and sits at the end of Main Street. The pool is fed by natural mineral hot springs and is open year-round.

than a billion years ago. Whole oceans have come and gone over hundreds of millions of years, leaving behind another 16,000 feet of sedimentary rock.

About 65 million years ago, the Rocky Mountains, including the San Juans, reared up. The San Juans were shaped in an elongate dome that straddles the boundary between two major geologic provinces—the Rocky Mountains and the Colorado Plateau.

From 40 to 25 million years ago, volcanoes repeatedly blew their stacks, coating the San Juans with igneous rocks, those born of fire. The garish reds and oranges and more subtle grays and purples capping many of the peaks are the cooled remnants of the lava and ash. About a million years ago glaciers added their artistic talent to the landscape, chiseling the skyline of the San Juan into sharp horns and arêtes and scooping out elegant cirques and U-shaped valleys. The last glaciers departed only about 10,000 to 15,000 years ago.

As so often happens, geology determines history and culture. During the volcanism, hot liquid shot up through fissures in the rocks of the San Juans. When the liquid cooled, gold, silver, lead, copper and zinc charted veins through the mountains. Much later, these would bring great riches to some people.

One of the first was Charles Baker, who in 1860 entered a big valley called Baker's Park on the west side of the San Juans. He was looking for gold, but instead found such profitable veins of silver that the town laid out in Baker's Park was soon bustling. Silverton supposedly got its name when a miner boasted, "We may not have gold here, but we have silver by the ton."

Soon the population of Silverton reached 3,000 and bars and saloons—40 of them—lined the main street. Even Wyatt Earp and Bat Masterson frequented the saloons at times. As the droves of miners entered, the only real threat they met, besides avalanches, fires and cave-ins, was the Ute Indians. The Utes once claimed nearly all of western Colorado, but in 1873 ceded millions of acres of the San Juans, opening the region to mining in return for an annual payment of $25,000.

The names of the mines—Expectation, Crown Jewel, Silver Peak, Last Dollar—hint at high hopes and final tries. In fact, the hills in the area have produced more than a quarter of a billion dollars' worth of gold, silver, lead, copper and zinc ore, but today, travelers in the San Juans see testimonies to those days in the weather-beaten, wooden mine shafts and rusted vehicles scattered everywhere throughout the mountains.

Most of the towns in the San Juans date to the mining days. Just beneath the peaks that hold the headwaters of the San Miguel River sits Telluride.

This town perhaps best illustrates the boom-and-bust cycle that brands San Juan Mountain communities. Gold was discovered here in 1875 and by 1878 the town was founded—named after an element called tellurium that is found with gold and silver deposits. The Sheridan, Tomboy, Smuggler-Union and Liberty Bell mines put Telluride on the map in the 1890's; some three dozen all-hour saloons were doing a roaring business. The town was a magnet for other activity as well. The infamous Butch Cassidy pulled off his very first successful bank robbery in Telluride in 1899. He and his companions held up the bank in broad daylight, then escaped by galloping their horses through the town.

But by the 1920's, the boom had gone bust as the veins played out and economic depression gripped the nation. Telluride languished into the 1970's, when many storefronts and homes were still boarded up.

TELLURIDE'S NEWEST BOOM

Today, the story has changed. A steady line of construction workers' pickups heads up along the San Miguel into town in the morning and back home in the afternoon. Telluride's new boom is fueled by construction of posh ski village condos just outside town and restoration of the fine Victorian homes on every street in town. Colorado Avenue, Telluride's main street, is lined with inns, restaurants, real estate offices, nightspots and

Letting the llamas carry the load is becoming an increasingly popular way for hikers to explore areas such as Bear Creek Basin. In Yankee Boy Basin, near Ouray, in the Uncompahgre National Forest, Rocky Mountain columbines (Colorado's state flower) and bright red Indian paintbrush thrive.

TUNDRA CARPET
Fragile alpine tundra covers sections of the La Plata Mountains in the Bear Creek Basin area of the San Juan National Forest, opposite page. Colorado is home to three-quarters of the U.S. land that is more than 10,000 feet above sea level.

upscale clothing stores. A full schedule of summer festivals—bluegrass, jazz, film, dance, chamber music and even a wild mushroom celebration—has made Telluride an international, year-round destination.

A perpetual problem during the first boom in the San Juans was how to get in and how to get out. Transportation was a constant concern: getting ore from the mines (often located above 11,000 feet) over the passes, to the nearest railhead, and on to the smelters. Likewise, food, mail, tools, timber and all other supplies had to be carted in to support the new towns; until the mid-20th century, all this was done on foot, burro, donkey or by oxen-drawn freight wagon. (One burro, legend tells it, traversed Engineer Mountain on snowshoes in 1879!)

The man who did the most to overcome the transportation obstacle was the "Pathfinder of the San Juans," Otto Mears. Born in Russia and orphaned at age four, Mears came to the United States and found his calling in life—transforming the dirt and avalanche-prone donkey trails of the San Juans into lucrative railroads and toll roads. He directed construction of the Million Dollar Highway, the narrow, winding, barely two-lane road that takes you through the San Juan Mountains for 70 breathtaking miles between Durango and Ouray.

| BUILDING A VERTICAL HIGHWAY |

In 1883, the editor of the *Solid Muldoon*, Ouray's newspaper, characterized the road as "four parts vertical and one part perpendicular." When people want to know how the Million Dollar Highway got its name, they have a choice of answers. Some say the road was paved with precious minerals; others

say it cost a million to build. The truth may exist in the statement of a contractor who, in the 1920's, referred to "this million dollar highway" he was helping build. In any case the Million Dollar Highway, U.S. Highway 550, was finally paved in the mid-1950's. Guardrails were installed, but most were later removed so that snowplows could push the drifts over the steep slope. With the amount of snow that falls each year in the San Juans, most wise drivers will realize that winter is not the time to drive the family sedan over this road without having chains on the tires.

From Ouray the Million Dollar Highway crosses Bear Creek Falls and passes under the recently completed Riverside avalanche shed. Had the shed been in place in 1965, it might have saved three lives. Three crosses stand beside the road in memory of Reverend Marvin Hudson and his daughters, Amelia and Pauline, who were killed on a Sunday in March by this perennial avalanche. Avalanches commonly slash through the San Juans, especially in the spring. Road signs that order "No Stopping or Standing" are there for a good reason.

Farther up the road in a wide-open park are the remains of the old mining town of Ironton. A few miles beyond, the Million Dollar Highway reach-

Abandoned mining buildings near Cinnamon Pass remain as reminders of the heyday of mining in the San Juan Mountains. Some of the area's diggings have been worked continuously since the 1870's; others were deserted in the 1890's when the federal government repealed an act that had subsidized the price of silver.

STEAM POWER

The Durango & Silverton Narrow Gauge Railroad, seen here crossing the Animas River heading toward Silverton, is one of the few remaining narrow-gauge railway lines in the Colorado mountains. The scenery along the 45-mile route through the San Juan National Forest is unforgettable.

es its highest point at Red Mountain Pass, 11,075 feet. It then begins a rapid descent along Mineral Creek into Silverton. Beavers have strung dams across the creek, and the spruce and fir trees beside the road are thick and beautiful. From Silverton you climb up and over two more 10,000-plus passes, Molas and Coal Bank, on the way into Durango.

The Million Dollar Highway is part of another, longer driving tour called the San Juan Skyway, a national forest and Colorado scenic and historic byway. ("Scenic," incidentally, is an understatement.) The Skyway is a 236-mile loop of paved highways. It heads west from Durango to Cortez, then north to Dolores, Telluride, and over the Dallas Divide to Ridgway, then south through Ouray, Silverton, and back to Durango. Visitors can drive it in a very long day, but they'd miss most of the attractions.

From Durango, a person might also head east on Highway 160 to Pagosa Springs, and continue on to Lake City on Highway 149. Or you could opt for a "shortcut" through the mountains from Ouray to Lake City called the Alpine Loop. This unpaved, backcountry byway (parts of it only negotiable by four-wheel drive) heads off just out of Ouray, climbs over 12,800-foot Engineer Pass, and drops into Lake City. The loop can be completed by going on to Silverton.

RELIVING THE DAYS OF STEAM

Besides auto touring, a sojourner in the San Juans has a choice of many other ways to see and enjoy the stunning mountains, depending upon the season and one's physical and mental state. You might jeep, hike, run, boat, fish, ski, cycle, tour a mine, climb an icefall or ride a llama. Or you can take a train.

More than 200,000 people view a glorious chunk of the San Juans each summer from the goldenrod-colored, 1880's-vintage coach cars of the Durango & Silverton Narrow Gauge Railroad. This coal-fired steam train, in operation for more than a century, blows its whistle and chuffs away from the Durango roundhouse each morning from May through October. It heads up through the pastoral Animas Valley, then enters the Animas Gorge.

The train slows to a crawl as it crosses a breathtaking wooden trestle hundreds of feet above the roaring river and passes through gaps so skinny you could reach out and touch the granite walls. About halfway up, backpackers can disembark at Needleton or Elk Park and head into the wilderness of the San Juans.

Most people, though, stay on the train as it heads for Silverton and lunch. After a couple of hours, the train leaves for the 45-mile trip back to Durango. The route, over which some $300 million in precious metals was hauled, can also be reversed by arrangement with the Silverton station master.

Durango bills itself as the "gateway" to the San Juans. Now a tourist and college town, it was founded in 1880 and served as a railroad and smelter town when mining hit the San Juans. There are some fine old hotels on Main Street— the town has two registered national historic districts with self-guided walking tours—and a lovely river walk along the Animas through town. Bodies clad in neon Lycra are evidence of Durango's growing reputation as the mountain-bike capital of Colorado.

Silverton, at the other end of the line, is downhome friendly. With 13,000-foot peaks looming on four sides, the town's setting is breathtaking. Due to its 9,320-foot elevation and geographical

location, Silverton boasts not one acre of agricultural land. Besides having lunch, visitors can also stroll down the infamous Blair Street. Admittedly this is now a tame experience compared to the heyday of mining, when Silverton's saloons, brothels and gambling halls (where Wyatt Earp dealt a few hands) served the rough-and-ready clientele.

For many years, Silverton's existence depended on the railway. During the winter months, heavy snowfall often cut the town off for days. Years ago, a train carrying passengers and freight was on its way to Silverton when a snowslide blocked the track. The people could not walk out, but fortunately did not have to go hungry. One freight car was filled with fresh eggs, so the passengers had eggs any way they liked them for the few days it took to clear the slide.

And then there's Ouray. You can reach this small town from Silverton on the Million Dollar Highway. Or you can approach from the west, over Dallas Divide, a drive so beautiful in autumn that you may have to pull off the road to let your emo-tions catch up with you. Either way you arrive, Ouray is a special destination. It was named after the Ute chief, Ouray. He was an articulate and charming man who spoke four languages and worked as a government interpreter. Known as a peacemaker and a tough negotiator, he helped work out the plan for the Ute to withdraw from the San Juan Mountains.

Today the town still has all the main street shops and quaint Victorian houses of other San Juan towns. But it's different. Small, warm yet sophisti-cated, Ouray is a town that knows who and what it wants to be.

Whether you've just jeeped over Imogene Pass from Telluride, hiked in Yankee Boy Basin, taken the historic walking tour in Ouray or camped in the Amphitheatre above town, there's still one last thing to do in Ouray. Go to the municipal pool at night for a soak in the therapeutic hot springs. Sheltered by the bulwarks of the mountains under impossibly bright stars, you may now be able to cope with ending your San Juan sojourn.

BOXED IN
The town of Telluride is settled into a box canyon almost 9,000 feet above sea level amid some of the loveliest, and wildest, landscape in the country. The town was founded in the 1870's by prospectors and still retains the flavor of a mining town, with its dirt streets and Victorian buildings. Today the town draws mountain climbers, hang gliders, skiers and film festival fans.

NEARBY SITES & ATTRACTIONS

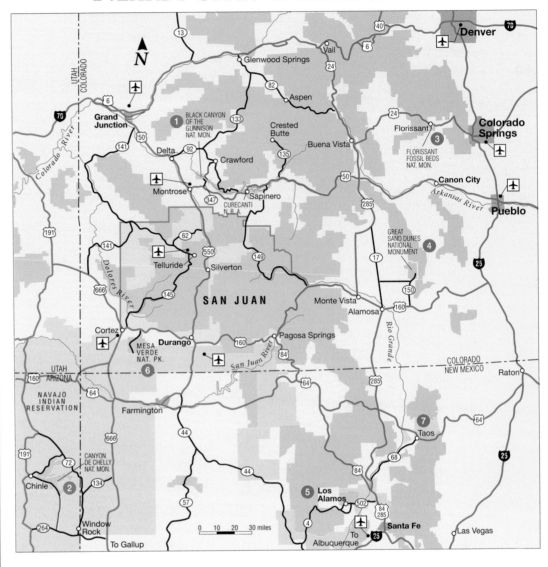

Adobe buildings in Taos recall traditional Pueblo Indian dwellings. The town's Plaza, heart of the original Spanish settlement, is still the focus of life in Taos.

The sands of the Great Sand Dunes National Monument are composed of eroded material carried by the Rio Grande from the San Juan Mountains long ago, and particles of rock left behind by glaciers.

① BLACK CANYON OF THE GUNNISON NATIONAL MONUMENT

Descending almost half a mile into the earth, the 53-mile-long rock cleft that scars the Gunnison National Monument area is so narrow and shadowy, and its walls are so steep, that 19th-century explorers called it the Black Canyon. The canyon was formed over a period of two million years as the Gunnison River cut through soft volcanic rock and then through deeper layers of hard schist and gneiss. Twelve miles of the most spectacular stretch are preserved in a wilderness state as part of the Black Canyon of the Gunnison National Monument. Scenic roads run along the north and south rims of the canyon, with overlooks such as Dragon Point and Narrows View affording matchless vistas of the canyon's beauty. Upstream, Curecanti National Recreation Area's three deep lakes were created when the Gunnison River was dammed. Together they provide abundant opportunities for boating, water sports and fishing. Located east of Montrose off Hwys. 50 and 347.

② CANYON DE CHELLY NATIONAL MONUMENT

This spectacular network of canyons was formed as streams cut their way through layers of sandstone deposited more than 200 million years ago. Canyon de Chelly's main tributary, Canyon del Muerto, takes its name from the remains of prehistoric Indian burials found there. The sheer walls of the canyon once sheltered the Anasazi, who built a number of cliff dwellings in recesses in the reddish stone. During the 1800's, Canyon de Chelly became a refuge for the Navajo people. Located in the Navajo Reservation, the site is today administered by the National Park Service. In summer, Navajo families still farm the fertile canyon bottomlands. For the best views of the canyon, drive along the North and South Rim Drives. Located outside Chinle off Hwy. 191.

③ FLORISSANT FOSSIL BEDS NATIONAL MONUMENT

Beneath the rolling meadows of a central Colorado valley, fossils preserved in the shale of an ancient lakebed have helped geologists to tell the story of the region during the Eocene Epoch, some 35 million years ago. Erosion has gradually exposed these fossil layers, revealing perfectly preserved leaves, insects, birds, mammals and fish. Many of these are displayed at the visitor center of this 6,000-acre site. One of the highlights of Florissant lakebed is a group of petrified sequoia tree stumps. The surrounding grasslands are rich in wildflowers and animal life, and there are 12 miles of hiking trails. Located off Hwy. 24, south of the town of Florissant.

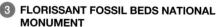

④ GREAT SAND DUNES NATIONAL MONUMENT

At the base of the Sangre de Cristo Mountains, a 39-square-mile expanse of sand dunes has been piled up by winds blowing across the San Luis Valley. At about 700 feet in height, these are the tallest sand dunes in North America. Once these sands lay on the bed of the Rio Grande. When the river changed course, the wind carried the exposed sand northeastward, until it was trapped by the mountains. The shape of the dune ridges changes daily as the wind slowly reshapes them; the mass itself is very stable. Great Sand Dunes National Monument preserves the main dune field—a total of 24,986 acres—as a wilderness area. Visitors can hike through the dunes, which are home to a surprising variety of plants and animals. Located off Hwy. 160, at the end of Hwy. 150.

⑤ LOS ALAMOS

During World War II, isolated Los Alamos Ranch School became the research headquarters of the Manhattan Project, which developed the first atomic bomb. Surrounded by forests of ponderosa pine, scores of scientists worked here under conditions of absolute secrecy, directed by Dr. J. Robert Oppenheimer. Today, the site remains an important center for scientific research. At the Bradbury Science Museum, exhibits tell the story of the Manhattan Project and explore new discoveries

in atomic energy and alternative energy sources. Located northwest of Santa Fe on Hwy. 502.

⑥ MESA VERDE NATIONAL PARK

The cliff dwellings of Mesa Verde, which can be seen by walking on two self-guided nature trails, were sighted in 1888 by two cowboys searching for cattle lost in a snowstorm. Mesa Verde National Park was created in 1906 to preserve the remarkable collection of buildings and structures found in the mesa country at the foot of the San Juan Mountains. These "apartment buildings" and villages were built by the Anasazi civilization, who abandoned the region around A.D. 1300, perhaps because of drought. The most famous site in the park is the Cliff Palace, which includes more than 200 stone rooms, as well as 23 kivas (sunken ceremonial rooms). The park is open all year round, but some sites are closed in winter. Located 35 miles west of Durango, off Hwy. 160.

⑦ TAOS

The town of Taos grew from a Spanish mission outpost set up close to historic Taos Pueblo in 1615. During the 1800's, fur traders and frontiersmen like Kit Carson flocked to the settlement. Artists and writers followed—Georgia O'Keeffe, D.H. Lawrence among them—attracted by the breathtaking scenery, clear air and the town's mix of Spanish, Indian and Anglo culture. Today Taos is still an artistic colony, and the nearby Taos Ski Valley and Sipapu Ski Area attract growing numbers of visitors each year. Historic sites include the home of Kit Carson, and the Martinez Hacienda, one of the few restored Spanish colonial residences in the nation. Located on Hwy. 64

The many-sided hogan, a type of log dwelling, is still used by the Navajo farmers who raise sheep and crops in Canyon de Chelly. The Anasazi, the earliest inhabitants of the canyons, grew corn and squash, and lived in circular pit houses dug into the earth.

The Trio, a group of adjoining petrified sequoia stumps, is one of the most famous of the fossil relics excavated at Florissant Fossil Beds National Monument.

THE WALLOWAS

The Wallowas? What's a Wallowa?
"Wall-oh-wuh"? "Wall-OH-wuh"?
"Wall-oh-WUH"?

That's "Wuh-LAO-uh," rhymes with "allow-a." Strictly speaking, the Wallowas are a mountain range in the northeast corner of Oregon, but the term "The Wallowas" has evolved into something more encompassing. Like other regions that derive their names from a mountain range—the Catskills or the Alps, for instance—the Wallowas include people, towns, foothills and valleys, and a characteristic way of life. Unlike the Catskills and the Alps, however, the Wallowas remain virtually unknown—maybe because no one knows how to pronounce their name.

The best way to explore the Wallowas is to travel between the towns of Wallowa and Halfway, with occasional side trips. This route takes in the Wallowa heartland: the mountain range itself, the Wallowa

Valley to the north, and a mosaic of Wallowa-Whitman National Forest, which includes Hells Canyon National Recreation Area to the east. Altogether that is about a million acres. The town of Wallowa seems like the appropriate place to begin a tour because of its name, but it is geography that dictates its status as the northern portal. The point where Highway 82 emerges from Minam Canyon, just west of town, marks the beginning of the Wallowa Valley. Grass-covered hills roll to a horizon sawed by mountain peaks. Isolated ranches speckle the landscape, their traditional red barns ablaze in the vivid sunlight.

After about eight miles the highway passes through Lostine, briefly serving as the main street of this little town of 230. Lostine fits into the surrounding ranchlands the way a pearl button fits into a

BACKCOUNTRY BYWAY
Along northeast Oregon's border with Washington, the majestic scenery of Buford Creek valley renders insignificant the contour-hugging Highway 3, barely visible on the right of this picture.

HAY HO!
Overleaf: Rolls of hay that look like huge loaves of fresh-baked bread crop up in the pastures of Wallowa County. The bounty of these grass-lands will see the livestock through the winter. Northeast Oregon is the state's most important grain-growing and ranching area.

cowboy shirt. A compelling side trip along the Lostine River leads due south from town. For a few miles the Lostine meanders through a gentle valley, then the river straightens and the valley narrows into a canyon as it climbs into the mountains. Conifer forests replace pastures and soon the road turns to gravel and dives into the national forest. About 10 miles from town, an overlook provides aerial views of this granite gash. In places the canyon is broad and the road swings close to river level, giving motorists easy access to the water should they feel the urge to skip stones or to slump in a shady glade and listen with closed eyes as the river whispers over the smooth rocks.

The end of the road provides access to the Eagle Cap Wilderness, a virtually unspoiled 360,000-acre enclave of dense forest, luxuriant meadows, glacial valleys and rough granite ridges. The Eagle Cap is renowned for its high alpine lakes: Legore Lake, at 8,880 feet above sea level, is the most elevated lake in Oregon. Backcountry visitors won't be alone up there. Deer, hawks and elk likely will put in appearances, while lucky observers may spot bighorn sheep, peregrine falcons, bald eagles and mountain goats. Some 500 miles of trails invite hikers, backpackers and horseback riders, but independent treks deep into the Eagle Cap are best left to the hardy and experienced. The less hardy and the inexperienced can sign up for guided trips on which packhorses or llamas shoulder the burden.

ENTER THE MOUNTAINS The high Wallowas form the backdrop to the south as tourists continue across the valley from Lostine. With each mile the mountains look higher and higher because the highway angles southeast toward them. By the time the highway metamorphoses into Main Street in downtown Joseph, the Eagle Cap Wilderness is only a few miles away and the mountains loom overhead. It is no wonder that one Joseph resident likens it to "living in a postcard."

Joseph was named after Chief Joseph, who led the Nez Perce during the 1870's. For generations the Nez Perce band had lived in the Wallowa Valley for part of the year, including summers spent in the Joseph area. They cherished this beautiful land, which they called "The Valley of the Winding Waters." When they made treaty concessions to the encroaching whites, Chief Joseph's band signed away other lands but clung to the valley. Only when the threat of military force became imminent did they reluctantly leave in 1877.

Driving into this town of 1,085 people, one might take it for another of the Wallowas' classic rural hamlets. That is partly accurate. Joseph has its share of garages decorated with elk antlers, welcoming

INFORMATION FOR VISITORS

Hwy. 84 provides access for the smaller highways that run through the Wallowas. The closest scheduled commercial air service is into Pendleton, Oregon, and Boise and Lewiston, Idaho. Full service charter aircraft services are available at Baker City and La Grande. The Wallowa Mountains Visitor Center, just outside Enterprise, provides information on the Wallowa-Whitman National Forest, including the Hells Canyon National Recreation Area. Some roads in the national forest are open seasonally; check road conditions before traveling. Commercial outfitters offer backcountry tours, including horse, llama and mule trips.
For more information: Eastern Oregon Visitors Association, P.O. Box 1087, Baker City, OR 97814. (503) 523-9200, (800) 332-1843; or Wallowa-Whitman National Forest, P.O. Box 907, 1550 Dewey Ave., Baker City, OR 97814. (503) 523-6391.

COUNTY SEAT
The sturdy Wallowa County Courthouse presides over Enterprise, the metropolis of the Wallowas, at 2,020 people. Though it is the largest town in the county, Enterprise handles its traffic problems without a single stoplight.

100

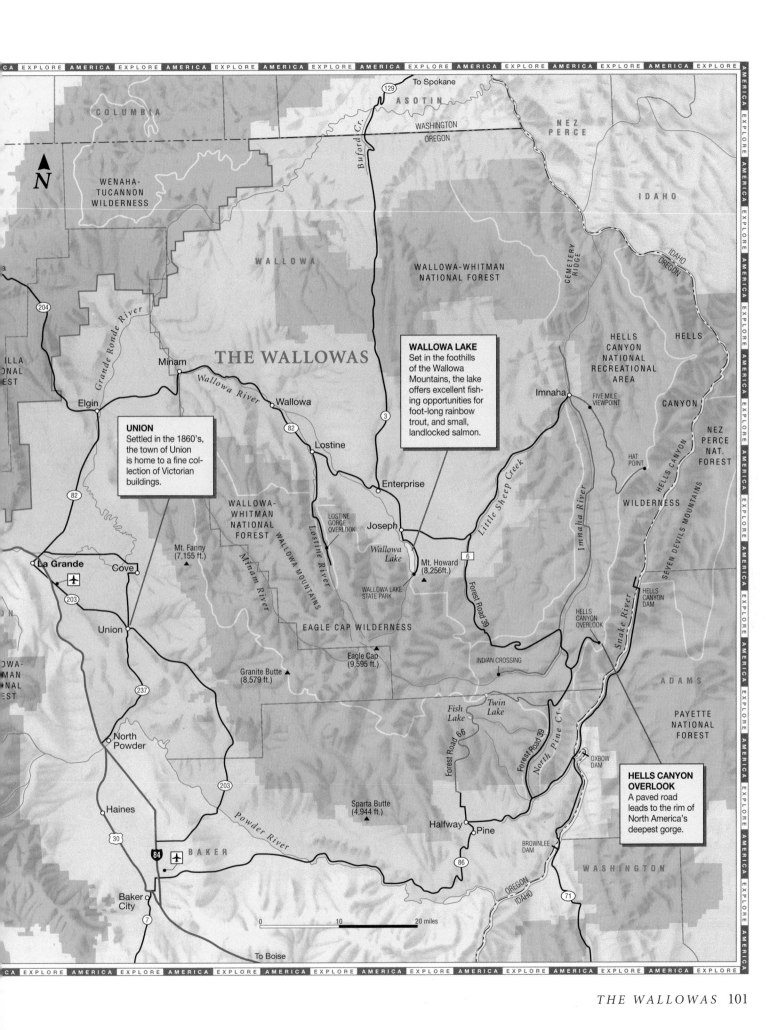

To Spokane

ASOTIN

COLUMBIA

WASHINGTON
OREGON

NEZ
PERCE

WENAHA-
TUCANNON
WILDERNESS

IDAHO

WALLOWA

WALLOWA-WHITMAN
NATIONAL FOREST

CEMETERY
RIDGE

Buford Cr.

IDAHO
OREGON

HELLS
CANYON
NATIONAL
RECREATIONAL
AREA

HELLS

THE WALLOWAS

Grande Ronde River

Minam

Wallowa River

Wallowa

Imnaha

FIVE MILE
VIEWPOINT

CANYON

Elgin

WALLOWA LAKE
Set in the foothills
of the Wallowa
Mountains, the lake
offers excellent fish-
ing opportunities for
foot-long rainbow
trout, and small,
landlocked salmon.

82

Lostine

NEZ
PERCE
NAT.
FOREST

HAT
POINT

Hells Canyon

UNION
Settled in the 1860's,
the town of Union
is home to a fine col-
lection of Victorian
buildings.

3

Enterprise

WILDERNESS

Little Sheep Creek

82

WALLOWA-
WHITMAN
NATIONAL
FOREST

LOSTINE
GORGE
OVERLOOK

Joseph

Imnaha River

HELLS CANYON

SEVEN DEVILS MOUNTAINS

Mt. Fanny
(7,155 ft.)

Lostine River

Wallowa
Lake

Mt. Howard
(8,256ft.)

6

HELLS
CANYON
OVERLOOK

HELLS
CANYON
DAM

La Grande

Cove

WALLOWA MOUNTAINS

Minam River

WALLOWA LAKE
STATE PARK

Forest Road 39

Snake River

203

Union

EAGLE CAP WILDERNESS

Eagle Cap
(9,595 ft.)

INDIAN CROSSING

ADAMS

237

Granite Butte
(8,579 ft.)

Twin
Lake

PAYETTE
NATIONAL
FOREST

North
Powder

Fish
Lake

Forest Road 66

Forest Road 39

North Pine Cr.

203

OXBOW
DAM

**HELLS CANYON
OVERLOOK**
A paved road
leads to the rim of
North America's
deepest gorge.

Haines

Sparta Butte
(4,944 ft.)

Halfway

Pine

30

Powder River

BROWNLEE
DAM

84

BAKER

WASHINGTON

86

Baker
City

OREGON
IDAHO

71

7

0   10   20 miles

To Boise

MARINE SURVIVOR
The rock debris found on some Wallowa slopes often yields fossils. These are ammonites, a family of long-extinct mollusks. Fossils like this were left behind when an ancient ocean covered these mountains about 300 to 130 million years ago.

CANYON GUARDIANS
Like a natural stone palisade, basalt columns brood over Imnaha Canyon in Hells Canyon National Recreation Area. These columns of hardened volcanic rock were formed roughly 16 million years ago, when lava flows covered the region.

front porches replete with wooden rockers, horses tossing their manes in backyard corrals, and tire swings dangling from big shade trees.

On closer inspection, the image of Joseph grows more complicated. A stroll down Main Street takes in a graceful sculpture of a deer, a tidy little museum and more art galleries than one would expect—lots more, considering that one would expect none. In fact, the town's largest employer (about 70 people) is Valley Bronze of Oregon, one of the finest bronze foundries in America.

A visit to Valley Bronze's Main Street showroom reveals what a splendid medium bronze can be. The gallery's ever-changing works may include a black hawk portrayed as mostly wings, or the lined face of a pioneer. A few blocks away at the foundry itself, tours take visitors through the whole magical process, from the artist's original sculpture to the pouring of the bronze and the coloring of the finished product. The tour also leads next door to the monument center, where artistic visions are realized on a grand scale. Visitors might see a worker tooling a 12-foot eagle or a snarling grizzly the size of a minivan. Another example of the foundry's artistry is the *Freedom Horses*, five exuberant 8-foot-tall and 12-foot-long horses depicted galloping over the fallen Berlin Wall.

Joseph's biggest bash is July's Chief Joseph Days, which revolves around a major rodeo. Some events are ongoing, such as summer's twice-weekly re-enactment of an 1896 bank robbery, staged in front of the very building where the crime originally occurred. Perhaps more impressive than all the gunfire and horsing around is the revelation that one of the robbers ended up as the vice-president of the bank.

TOWERING ATTRACTIONS At the south end of Wallowa Lake, six miles from Joseph, lie historic Wallowa Lake Lodge and Wallowa Lake State Park. From here, outfitters offer riding or horsepacking trips into the adjacent mountains. Towering above all the attractions, literally, is the tramway, reputedly the steepest in North America. It transports passengers 3,800 vertical feet to the summit of Mt. Howard for endless views of the lake, the valley and the Eagle Cap Wilderness.

Just east of Joseph a major side trip beckons. Thirty-three miles of pleasant motoring, most of it along picturesque Little Sheep Creek, leads to Imnaha. Too small to have a gas station, this town does manage to support a saloon. But Imnaha is just the jump-off point for a narrow, precipitous, gravel road that slithers 23 miles to Hat Point.

The road starts in high-desert canyon country, curving up past grassy slopes and rocky outcrops. After a few miles the road emerges from the hills and inches along a mountainside high above the Imnaha River canyon. By Five-Mile Viewpoint, travelers have ascended 2,655 feet. Presently, the route enters conifer forest as it tightropes along a ridge. A number of pullouts offer superb views of the Imnaha, but none prepares people for the vista from Hat Point itself, which is on a par with the Grand Canyon.

Comparing this view to that of the Grand Canyon may sound a bit inaccurate, and it is—the panorama from Hat Point is even more grand. It looks over Hells Canyon, the deepest gorge on the continent, beating out the Grand Canyon by some 1,500 to 2,000 feet. More than a vertical mile below Hat Point, the Snake River surges north, ceaselessly carving deeper and deeper. Across the river lies Idaho, where layers of mountain ridges culminate in the 9,000-foot-plus peaks of the Seven Devils Mountains, effectively the east rim. For the ultimate view, those with no fear of heights can climb the fire tower that crowns Hat Point. From there they can see furrowed canyon country and forested mountains fanning out to the curve of the Earth.

Back from the long side trip, motorists can continue on the Wallowas' main line by heading up

JOSEPH'S TOWN
The quiet little town of Joseph, named for the famed Nez Perce chief, seems to slumber in the morning sun. During the weekend-long Chief Joseph Days, held annually on the last full weekend in July, the town features a traditional Indian dance contest, a rodeo and parades.

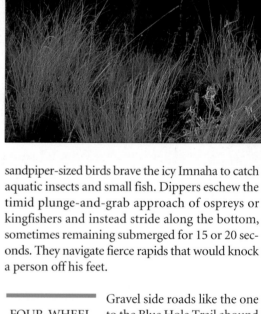

VALLEY GRAZING
Rugged Wallowa Valley horses graze near the tiny town of Lostine. Horseback riding is a popular way of exploring the mountains and meadows of the nearby Eagle Cap Wilderness.

Forest Road 39 (paved) for the 60-mile run to Halfway. Much of this is ponderosa pine territory. These mighty trees grow widely spaced, so hiking cross-country among them is like taking a walk in the park. Soon the road enters the Canal Fire area, where a huge conflagration seared 23,000 acres in 1989. Most of the trees are still standing, so for several miles the road is flanked by an eerie assemblage of gray-black skeletons—the scorched trunks and branches left behind after the needles and bark burned away. But fire doesn't destroy forests; it's merely a stage they go through periodically. A stroll in the burn reveals lodgepole pine seedlings amid the charred debris, a promise for the future.

Choosing a hike in the Wallowas is difficult. But a short side trip off Forest Road 39 to the Indian Crossing campground brings would-be trekkers to the Blue Hole Trail, a choice that has one advantage over most of its kin: it's nearly flat. It follows the Imnaha River up to the narrow, 100-foot-deep granite gorge that is the eponymous blue hole. The river's prancing waters provide almost constant, buoyant companionship to those walking the trail. The water is icy cold, but the dippers don't seem to mind. Properly labeled American dippers, these

sandpiper-sized birds brave the icy Imnaha to catch aquatic insects and small fish. Dippers eschew the timid plunge-and-grab approach of ospreys or kingfishers and instead stride along the bottom, sometimes remaining submerged for 15 or 20 seconds. They navigate fierce rapids that would knock a person off his feet.

FOUR-WHEEL DRIVES Gravel side roads like the one to the Blue Hole Trail abound along the middle stretch of Forest Road 39. Smaller side roads often branch off from those first side roads, and yet smaller roads branch off those second roads, and so forth, like a network of blood vessels. Some are primitive tracks that would be lethal to passenger cars, but many can be negotiated without four-wheel drive or high clearance if a driver is willing to go slowly. And who would want to drive fast along these scenic forest service backroads? Forest Road 66 is a classic example. It threads

through old-growth ponderosa pine, skirts Fish Lake and Twin Lakes, and provides view after view as it wriggles down the south side of the Wallowas.

Forest Road 3965 used to be another classic example, but in 1992 the Forest Service paved the first three miles. They had good reason. At the end of those three miles is their new Hells Canyon Overlook, where the views almost rise to the level of Hat Point—and they're an awful lot easier to get to. Late-afternoon visitors can sit at picnic tables and watch the setting sun's rays climb up the canyon, leaving the deep clefts in shadow while the high ground glows in the rich light.

As Forest Road 39 curves south down North Pine Creek, the grip of the Wallowas begins slipping. The ponderosa gradually are replaced by deciduous trees (the creek is a riot of yellow and gold in autumn) and the mountains melt into hills. But just before the Wallowas fade out, the road intersects Highway 86, where a westward turn leads to Halfway, the southern portal to the Wallowas.

A rumpled little town with a tidy white church, and a few fences between neighbors, Halfway rests in lush Pine Valley under the spell of the mountains. Its setting is like Wallowa's, except the range lies to the north instead of to the south. Halfway and Pine Valley are reminiscent of Wallowa and the Wallowa Valley in character, as well. The ranches, the barns, the hay loaves, the cattle; the details are the same right down to the tire swings.

Travelers heading on down Highway 86 out of Halfway and out of the Wallowas should pull off at the summit about four miles south of town and look back. In the foreground the tall grasses growing between the clumps of sagebrush sway in the breeze. In the background the pinnacles of the Wallowas aspire to the sky. And in the middle ground smiles Pine Valley, green and fertile, neck-laced by tree-lined creeks. In those old Westerns when the hero wistfully spoke of settling down someday on a little spread somewhere, this surely is the kind of somewhere he had in mind.

CANYON CREST

The view from Cemetery Ridge, near the confluence of the Imnaha and Snake Rivers, out over the rugged Hells Canyon Recreation Area, seems to go on forever. Hells Canyon hugs the borders of north-east Oregon and Idaho and is the deepest river gorge in the U.S.

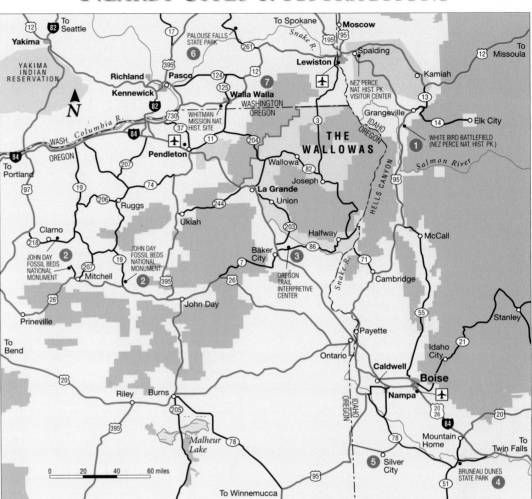

Palouse Falls plunges suddenly from a rocky gorge into a rimrock basin below. Downstream from the falls, caves in the base of the canyon were used by the Palouse Indians for shelter and storage. The gently rolling Palouse hills lie to the east of this state park.

NEARBY SITES & ATTRACTIONS

① NEZ PERCE NATIONAL HISTORICAL PARK

The park preserves the culture and history of the Nez Perce Indians, and consists of 38 separate sites, most in north-central Idaho. The visitor center in Spalding also houses the Museum of Nez Perce Culture. Sites of interest include the Nimipu Trail, followed by Lewis and Clark on their 1805 expedition; and White Bird Battlefield, the location of the first battle of the Nez Perce War of 1877. Hwys. 12 and 95 are the main routes to the sites.

② JOHN DAY FOSSIL BEDS NATIONAL MONUMENT

This site chronicles a climatic change that took place 5 to 50 million years ago—the transition from a tropical environment to high desert. Flora and fauna from this period have been preserved as fossils within this national monument. The site encompasses three units—Sheep Rock, Painted Hills and Clarno; trails meander through some of the sites; signs along the way explain the fossils. There is a visitor center at Sheep Rock located on Hwy. 19; Painted Hills is 6 miles north of Hwy. 26; Clarno is on Hwy. 218.

③ OREGON TRAIL INTERPRETIVE CENTER

The Oregon Trail snaked westward from Independence, Missouri, to Oregon City, Oregon, a distance of over 2,000 miles. From 1841 to 1861, 300,000 emigrants trekked over deserts, prairies and mountain ranges along this frontier route. The center is located near Baker City—once an important halt on the Trail. The museum displays artifacts, photographs, letters and diaries, and recreates the sights and sounds of the Trail in a 100-foot-long gallery. Outdoor displays include a pioneer encampment and a gold mining camp. Visitors can hike along 5 miles of interpretive trails, where original pioneer wagon ruts can still be seen. Located on Flagstaff Hill, east of Baker City on Hwy. 86.

④ BRUNEAU DUNES STATE PARK

Marooned incongruously in the midst of the lakes and marshland of southern Idaho are two huge sand dunes. These mountains cover around 600 acres of this 4,800-acre preserve, and the tallest of the two stands some 470 feet high. Local wind conditions permitted sand to accumulate in this hollow along the Snake River. The same conditions trapped the dunes, and kept them from moving. In May and

The banded sediments of the Painted Hills unit of John Day Fossil Beds were laid down roughly 30 million years ago. At that time, frequent volcanic eruptions showered ash over the region, preserving wood, leaves and animals. Erosion has exposed these layers, which take their colors from the presence of various minerals.

June, a carpet of wildflowers blooms at the base of the dunes, which are also home to numerous coyotes. The surrounding wetlands were created when a nearby reservoir caused the water table to rise. The marshes support extensive waterfowl and provide superb fishing. Located 20 miles south of Mountain Home off Hwy. 51.

5 SILVER CITY

In 1862 prospectors found gold in Jordan Creek, in the Owyhee Mountains. The treasure seekers also found large slabs of silver, after which they named the town which sprang up in this mountain hollow. Today, 70 buildings in Silver City Historic District remain from the town's glory days. The surrounding area is rich in abandoned mines and ghost towns. Silver City is a tiny living community. Visitors can stay in the Idaho Hotel, a five-story survivor from the 1860's, complete with original furnishings (no electricity, but solar lighting). Located 23 miles southwest of Hwy. 78 (check road conditions Oct.-May).

6 PALOUSE FALLS STATE PARK

The Palouse River plunges over the edge of a plateau in a 195-foot waterfall, and then rushes 8 miles through a narrow canyon on its way to join the Snake River. Palouse Falls ranks as one of the most spectacular natural wonders in a state renowned for its scenic beauty. At Palouse Falls State Park, visitors can hike to the top of the plateau for a view of the falls, or descend to the swirling horseshoe-shaped pool at its foot. Owls are among the many bird species that nest in the cliffs. Located off Hwy. 261.

7 WALLA WALLA

Built on an old Indian trail, Walla Walla later became a welcome halt on the Oregon Trail. Walla Walla, which means "many waters" in Nez Perce, is home to the Fort Walla Walla Museum Complex, a recreated pioneer village. The Whitman Mission National Historic Site, located 7 miles west of the city, preserves the site of Washington's first Protestant mission, established in 1836 by Dr. Marcus Whitman and his wife. Markers show the outlines of the mission's buildings, destroyed in 1847 by the Cayuse Indians. Located at the junction of Hwys. 12 and 125.

In its heyday, Silver City was one of the richest mining towns in the West. Its mines yielded a staggering $60 million in gold and silver. When the gold and silver ran out, the miners moved on, and the town quietly slipped into dereliction.

MENDOCINO COUNTY

---

*Its rugged coastline contrasts
with the rolling hills and
vine-laden valleys of the interior.*

The forever view from the top of the Point Arena Lighthouse reveals the essence of Mendocino County's dual nature. Just north, white-maned waves burst into a glittering mist against the chests of the sea cliffs, while on the grassy flats above the cliffs dairy cows placidly graze. Just south, harbor seals and husky Stellar's sea lions bark and bicker on the rocky shore, while diners in Point Arena Harbor restaurants sip wine and eavesdrop on those boisterous pinnipeds. A few miles up the coast in the little town of Elk, guests at several fashionable inns look out their windows and watch the cormorants, murres and pigeon guillemots nesting on the sea stacks just offshore. Everything in sight, except the open Pacific, suggests the balance between the wild and the developed that typifies this northern California county.

Mendocino County lies at a confluence. To the south sprawl San Francisco and the nearby counties that spin within its urban orbit. To the north stretch the wild places of Humboldt and Del

Norte Counties and southern Oregon. And where the currents meet one finds Mendocino County—not predominantly civilized, not predominantly natural, but a captivating blend of both.

That blend is most evident on the Mendocino coast. As travelers meander along shore-hugging Highway 1, they discover the route's alternating rhythm: a small town or a relatively densely settled rural area followed by a natural preserve, followed by another settlement, then another preserve, and so forth. The only exception to this pattern is found in the extreme north, where Highway 1 flees inland to avoid the impassably savage terrain of the last 20 miles of the Mendocino coastline.

Most of this rugged northern region falls inside the boundaries of Sinkyone Wilderness State Park. Travelers willing to brave the seasonal dirt access road and the steep trails can enter a land of raw gorges, forested knife-edge ridges, black-sand beaches, and shore-front mountains that thrust from the ocean on a rocket's trajectory.

More typical of Mendocino's beach preserves is MacKerricher State Park, which harbors eight miles of undeveloped shoreline between Fort Bragg and Ten Mile River. Any time is a good time to watch long combers curl onto a dune-backed beach or to stand atop a rocky point as fierce breakers rattle the earth, but early morning is special at MacKerricher. That's when Lake Cleone comes alive, for one thing. A former tidal lagoon now cut off from the sea, the lake brims with bird life. A stroll along the boardwalk that borders Lake Cleone may yield sightings of herons and white-plumed egrets mincing about in the shallows on their stilt-like legs, dabbling mallards upending in the water to nibble submerged grasses, and ospreys hovering low over the marshes in search of prey.

But the siren call of the sea soon lures most visitors to the adjacent shore. Some wander the ocean's margin, fondling shells and admiring the peachy glow of the sand as it glistens in the low-angled morning sunlight. Others take to the dunes, where that same light paints rippling shadow-stripes on the tawny sand and awakens the colors of the beach morning glory, sand verbena and coast paintbrush. Those visitors who want to go to sea without a boat can venture far out to the tip of Laguna Point on a boardwalk trail. Fog may cast its net across the bay to the north, while the harbor seals in the rookery to the south may be moaning and groaning as they rouse themselves.

Low tide is another special time at MacKerricher. The receding waters unveil the thronged world of the rocky intertidal zone. Vast assemblages of barnacles cling to the sides of the rocks. Fiddler crabs scuttle across the bottoms of limpid tidepools. Predatory sea stars (starfish) drape their purple, orange or tan forms over mussels and slowly pry the shells open.

Just a few miles on the other side of Fort Bragg from MacKerricher, coastal travelers encounter Jughandle State Reserve, an example of the other form taken by Mendocino coastal parks. Like MacKerricher, Jughandle is long and narrow, but its length stretches several miles inland rather than along the shore. This orientation means that Jug Handle and its brethren, Russian Gulch and Van Damme State Parks, take visitors on a journey from the coast up into the forested hills.

ECOLOGICAL STAIRCASE

Jughandle stands out as an opportunity to make the acquaintance of the ecosystem behind the beaches because of the self-guided nature trail that leads up the "ecological staircase." The staircase consists of terraces that have been formed by wave actions during the last half-million years as sea levels rose and fell. Now, at the rate of an inch a century, they are being uplifted. Five are exposed and ready for inspection by hikers and a sixth is on its gradual way. Each terrace is 100,000 years older and 100 feet higher than the one below it and each harbors different plant and animal communities.

The trail starts amid the poppies and paintbrush of the coastal prairie. From there it ascends into the krummholz, the wind-battered forest of short, bent, tormented trees. After lush creek canyon, the trail rises into a forest of fir, hemlock, pine and spruce. Finally, it leads to vaulting groves of redwoods and Douglas firs—but not without a strange

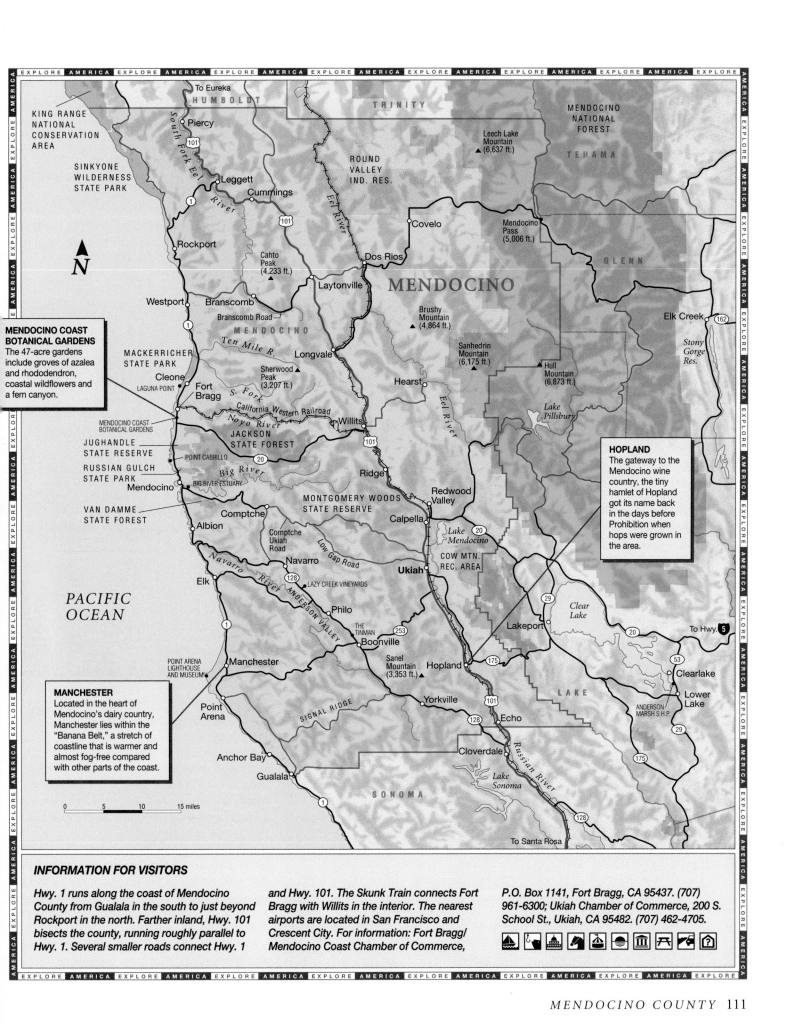

EXPLORE AMERICA EXPLORE AMERICA EXPLORE AMERICA EXPLORE AMERICA EXPLORE AMERICA EXPLORE AMERICA EXPLORE AMERICA EXPLORE

To Eureka

HUMBOLDT

TRINITY

MENDOCINO NATIONAL FOREST

KING RANGE NATIONAL CONSERVATION AREA

Piercy

Leech Lake Mountain (6,637 ft.) ▲

TEHAMA

South Fork Eel River

SINKYONE WILDERNESS STATE PARK

Leggett

Cummings

ROUND VALLEY IND. RES.

Covelo

Mendocino Pass (5,006 ft.)

GLENN

Rockport

Eel River

Dos Rios

MENDOCINO COAST BOTANICAL GARDENS
The 47-acre gardens include groves of azalea and rhododendron, coastal wildflowers and a fern canyon.

Westport

Cahto Peak (4,233 ft.) ▲

Branscomb

Branscomb Road

MENDOCINO

Laytonville

MENDOCINO

Elk Creek

162

Brushy Mountain (4,864 ft.) ▲

Stony Gorge Res.

Ten Mile R.

Longvale

Sanhedrin Mountain (6,175 ft.) ▲

Hull Mountain (6,873 ft.) ▲

MACKERRICHER STATE PARK

Sherwood Peak (3,207 ft.) ▲

Hearst

Cleone

LAGUNA POINT

Fort Bragg

S. Fork

California Western Railroad

Noyo River

JACKSON STATE FOREST

Willits

Lake Pillsbury

Eel River

MENDOCINO COAST BOTANICAL GARDENS

JUGHANDLE STATE RESERVE

POINT CABRILLO

20

101

Ridge

HOPLAND
The gateway to the Mendocino wine country, the tiny hamlet of Hopland got its name back in the days before Prohibition when hops were grown in the area.

RUSSIAN GULCH STATE PARK

Big River

Mendocino

BIG RIVER ESTUARY

MONTGOMERY WOODS STATE RESERVE

Redwood Valley

VAN DAMME STATE FOREST

Comptche

Calpella

Lake Mendocino

20

Albion

Comptche Ukiah Road

COW MTN. REC. AREA

PACIFIC OCEAN

Navarro River

Low Gap Road

Ukiah

Navarro

128

LAZY CREEK VINEYARDS

ANDERSON VALLEY

Clear Lake

29

Elk

Philo

Lakeport

20

To Hwy. 5

THE TINMAN

253

175

53

Boonville

Sanel Mountain (3,353 ft.) ▲

Hopland

Clearlake

MANCHESTER
Located in the heart of Mendocino's dairy country, Manchester lies within the "Banana Belt," a stretch of coastline that is warmer and almost fog-free compared with other parts of the coast.

POINT ARENA LIGHTHOUSE AND MUSEUM

Manchester

Yorkville

LAKE

ANDERSON MARSH S.H.P.

Lower Lake

29

101

Point Arena

SIGNAL RIDGE

128

Echo

Russian River

Cloverdale

Lake Sonoma

Anchor Bay

1

Gualala

SONOMA

175

128

0 5 10 15 miles

To Santa Rosa

INFORMATION FOR VISITORS

Hwy. 1 runs along the coast of Mendocino County from Gualala in the south to just beyond Rockport in the north. Farther inland, Hwy. 101 bisects the county, running roughly parallel to Hwy. 1. Several smaller roads connect Hwy. 1

and Hwy. 101. The Skunk Train connects Fort Bragg with Willits in the interior. The nearest airports are located in San Francisco and Crescent City. For information: Fort Bragg/ Mendocino Coast Chamber of Commerce,

P.O. Box 1141, Fort Bragg, CA 95437. (707) 961-6300; Ukiah Chamber of Commerce, 200 S. School St., Ukiah, CA 95482. (707) 462-4705.

MENDOCINO COUNTY 111

SEASIDE CHARM

Early morning fog drifts in and envelops the town of Mendocino. This quaint village sits atop rugged bluffs overlooking the Pacific Ocean. The New England-style architecture is the work of homesick northeasterners who were drawn here during the town's lumber boom. The town became a favorite with artists during the late 1950's. The tranquillity of the village is apparent, below, where an on-duty fireman puts his feet up in the shade of Mendocino's firehouse.

interruption from a pygmy forest. In this Lilliputian woods, stunted pines and cypresses languish in gray, nutrient-poor soil almost as acidic as vinegar. Mature trees that would have grown taller than 100 feet in ordinary soil may be only a foot high.

Parks dominate the natural-area itineraries of most travelers along the Mendocino coast, but some of its outdoor treasures aren't shaded in on the maps as are the designated nature preserves. The Big River estuary, for instance. One of the largest relatively undisturbed estuaries in California, this tidal stretch of Big River extends inland for more than eight miles. It's made to order for exploration in canoes or kayaks, which can be rented right at the river's mouth.

Salt marshes line the lower section of the estuary. Paddlers can glide by or even strike out into the marshes via narrow channels for a close-up

look at herons, egrets and other marsh wildlife. Farther upriver the marshes give way to conifer forests. Kingfishers flash up and down the banks, emitting their raucous, rattling calls. Sometimes deer show up to get a drink; occasionally they even startle onlookers by swimming across the river. Frequently, river otters slide into view, curving through the water with sinewy grace. The fearless otter young sometimes swim right up to canoes. Travelers concerned about the rigors of paddling upriver needn't worry if they time their outing properly; they can go up with the tide, turn when the tide turns, and come back down with the tide. Barring headwinds, canoeists theoretically could make a slow round trip without taking a single stroke of the paddles.

One of the Mendocino coast's most engaging natural phenomena doesn't show up on the map at all. To enjoy it, travelers need only find some high ground with an ocean view and watch for the spouts of the California gray whales. They stream past by the thousands during their migration between their Arctic feeding grounds and their Baja California breeding lagoons. These leviathans appear during March, April and May on their way north, but they pass closer to shore—sometimes only 400 to 800 yards offshore—and in greater concentrations during their southbound voyage in December and January. To celebrate the migration, the towns of Mendocino, Gualala and Fort Bragg stage whale festivals every year on the first, second and third weekends in March.

Given the Mendocino coast's natural endowments, it's no surprise that European civilization first came to these shores in order to convert that natural wealth into personal wealth. In 1850 a crew was sent from San Francisco to salvage the cargo of a ship that had run aground off Point Cabrillo, but they forgot all about their salvage operation when they saw the vast redwood forests. The demand ignited by the California gold rush had made timber almost as valuable as gold itself, and within a decade, lumber mills were sawing away up and down the Mendocino coast. Several of today's quiet little hamlets were boisterous boom towns from the mid-1850's to the early 1900's. Tiny Westport, for example, was the largest seaport between San Francisco and Eureka during the 1880's, when 14 hotels and 17 saloons enlivened its streets. The only evidence today of those heady times is a handful

LOGS AND LIGHTS
Lumber schooners plying the
Northern California coast looked to
Point Cabrillo Lighthouse to guide
them through the thick coastal fog.
The structure was built in 1909.

of historic buildings and the rusting remains of the cables and chains from a long-gone wharf.

Most Mendocino coastal lumber towns followed Westport's pattern of boom and bust, but there were two notable exceptions: Fort Bragg and the town of Mendocino. Fort Bragg has grown into the Mendocino coast's largest city (though it's hardly large, with a population of about 6,000) by remaining a lumber center while attracting lots of tourists with its inns, restaurants and galleries. Fort Bragg also benefits from the presence of Noyo Harbor just south of town, home to the county's largest commercial fishing fleet. Even people who aren't bringing in a load of cod should plot a course to the harbor. They can watch the fishers unloading their catch, feast on fresh seafood in dockside restaurants, shop at the fish markets, or simply laze on the pier and take in the boat traffic.

The town of Mendocino took a different route from lumber bust to present prosperity. Mendocino generally does things differently. This village of 1,200 souls started metamorphosing into a free spirit when artists began trickling into town during the 1950's to take advantage of its inspirational beauty—and the low housing prices that followed the demise of the local lumber mills. (Ironically, the revival of Mendocino initiated by the artists has led to six-digit housing prices.) When developers tried to make over Mendocino in the 1970's, it was the art community that rallied to save the town and have it declared a National Historic Preservation District. Thank goodness they did. Now travelers can amble past gingerbread Victorian houses, the handsome old hotel, the 1867-vintage Presbyterian church and a plethora of old-fashioned inns. Two of the town's finest historic buildings, the Kelley House and the Ford House, serve as museums.

But Mendocino's present is at least as fascinating as its past, though in ways the two are inseparable. Art still pervades the community. Some of the putative galleries are little more than glorified souvenir shops, but many others are the real thing and display work many notches above the humdrum seascapes one might dread. The town's artistic hub is the Mendocino Art Center, founded in 1959. Visitors can contemplate the sculptures that grace the grounds; watch potters, weavers and other artists as they give form to their ideas; or wander through the gallery, which might display anything from traditional oil paintings to innovative works on mushroom paper.

Mendocino may be the epicenter of the area's artistic activity, but art flourishes everywhere on the coast. Settlements too small to have a gas station often have a gallery—or two. The artists themselves are scattered in hideaways all over the map.

HEADING FOR THE HILLS

Ferreting out artists' studios sometimes takes travelers east. This is one way in which they discover that there's more to Mendocino County than its 100-mile coastline—on average, the county also extends inland for about 40 miles. Literally and figuratively, Mendocino County is by no means one-dimensional.

A number of alluring back roads lead into the interior. Typical is the Comptche-Ukiah Road, which winds from Mendocino to Ukiah. Motorists head for the hills at 20 or 30 miles per hour, passing from the mixed conifer and redwood forests

near the coast to the oak-conifer woodlands farther inland to the oak-grasslands of Mendocino County's eastern hemisphere. Sometimes the road is a tunnel overgrown by trees. Other times it climbs high up an open hillside for expansive vistas of the hills and valleys. About the only signs of humanity are a scattering of cabins, a few ranches and the minuscule town of Comptche, which is anchored by a comely little redwood church.

The California Western Railroad also leads into the interior, hauling passengers between Fort Bragg and Willits. However, anyone who asks for the California Western Railroad will only get blank looks from locals. This line is universally known as the "Skunk Train," a name bestowed on the malodorous gas-engine rail cars that plied the route years ago. Inaugurated as a logging railroad in 1885, the Skunk is primarily a tourist train today, though it still delivers mail and supplies to isolated outposts. Passengers travel in open observation cars that afford clear views of the redwoods, the ranches, the Noyo River and the sinuous hills.

The appeal of inland Mendocino County lies not only in the getting there, but in the places travelers can get to. The same blend of civilization and nature that characterizes the coast also is evident in the interior. Scenic drives and hikes await in the Mendocino National Forest, Jackson State Forest,

Mendocino County has been producing world-class wines ever since the first winery opened in 1879. The county's wine-growing regions are divided into six valleys, each of which yields different types of grapes because of slight variations in climate.

Majestic Monterey pine trees overlook the Pacific Ocean at Russian Gulch State Park. This evergreen tree, which grows to an average height of 100 feet, is native to Southern California. Its bright green needles are about six inches long.

and the Cow Mountain Recreation Area. Arguably, the most enchanting inland wild places are the pockets of old-growth redwoods, exemplified by Montgomery Woods State Reserve. Never logged, these ancient groves of trees still harbor giants. Thousands of years old and more than 300 feet tall, these arboreal elders convince onlookers that redwoods are the tallest trees in the world—which they are.

Civilization is more apparent in the interior than on the coast because of the development along the Highway 101 corridor. Generally, the Highway 101 towns lack the charm and character of their coastal cousins, but they have their moments. Take Ukiah, the county seat and Mendocino's largest city. (The greater Ukiah area's population of about 32,000 actually feels big after one has been in the area for a while.) Tucked away on a large lot in the middle of downtown are the Grace Hudson Museum and the Sun House. The handsome museum houses anthropology, history and art collections, mainly from the locally prominent Hudson family. Next to the museum is the Sun House, the Craftsman-style former residence built in 1911 by Grace and her husband, John. Fashioned from richly gleaming redwood, this simple, six-room bungalow demonstrates that scrupulous workmanship can be more attractive than opulence.

Travelers who roam about an hour northwest of 101 on pretty Highway 128 will meet up with the interior town richest in character—much of it eccentric. That would be Boonville. Its reputation for eccentricity largely stems from the fact that many of its residents used to "harp Boontling"— that is, they spoke a local language called "Boontling." Residents apparently concocted Boontling so they could speak privately to each other in the presence of outsiders. Though Boontling's heyday was between 1880 and 1920, the lingo still crops up around town, most prominently at the Horn of Zeese Coffee Shop. "Horn of zeese" means cup of coffee in Boontling. A lot of the menu is in Boontling, tempting customers with "boarf boos" (french fries), "fog eaters special" (fish and chips) and "borp slibs" (bacon). On the street outside there's even a phone booth bearing the Boontling name for public telephone, "buckey walter."

But Boonville is more than just an oddity. It also features a fine old hotel and restaurant, a brew pub, and, most notably, each September Boonville hosts the Mendocino County Fair and Apple Show. The fair is a wonderfully down-home celebration that includes a rodeo, sheepdog trials, produce displays and food booths.

Boonville is an apt location for showing off Mendocino's agriculture because the town lies in the verdant Anderson Valley. This pastoral pock-

et on the Navarro River is famed for its apples and grapes, and travelers can partake of both. In the late summer and fall, apples, some three dozen varieties, dominate the valley's produce stands.

Visitors also can sample cider and juice at roadside outlets. And, of course, many winery tasting rooms line Highway 128. During the last couple of decades, the Anderson Valley has come into its own as a wine-making region, receiving its appellation in 1983. In the stretch of highway between Philo and Navarro the tasting rooms appear at an average rate of about one per mile.

For a more intimate view of Anderson Valley wineries, travelers can make appointments to visit some of the small operations off the main drag. Strolling through the acres of vineyards is like walking through an exquisite formal garden and a pristine river valley at the same time. Green rows of grapes stripe large patches of the surrounding hills. Lower in the valley, golden sunlight pours through apple orchards whose trees are heavy with fruit of a color much like the sunlight. Redwoods and oaks swathe the higher slopes of the hills and mountains that frame the valley.

In this place, as in many places in Mendocino, the county's signature combination of civilization and nature has evolved beyond mere juxtaposition. The two elements have bonded together and become indivisible. The resulting chemistry is likely to produce a strong reaction in visitors, making them yearn to trade in their Calvin Kleins for an old pair of overalls.

NEARBY SITES & ATTRACTIONS

The wooden buildings that make up Fort Ross are modern reconstructions. The originals were erected by the Russians in 1812. The Orthodox Chapel, seen above, was destroyed by fire in 1971 and later rebuilt. The fort served as a supply depot and trading center and was never used for military operations.

Fishermen try their luck at Point Reyes. Spanish explorer Don Sebastían Vizcaíno sailed past the peninsula on January 6, 1603, and named it La Punta de Los Reyes to commemorate the day—the Feast of the Three Kings.

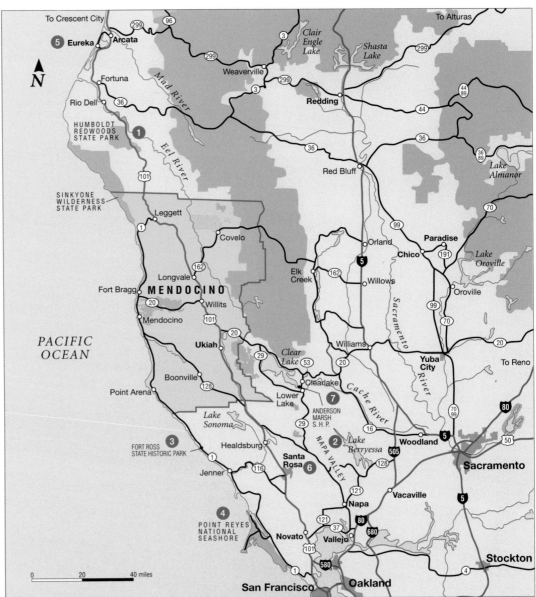

① HUMBOLDT REDWOODS STATE PARK

Many of the world's tallest coastal redwood trees, some of which reach 350 feet, grow along a 500-mile strip of the California coast. Some of the biggest are in the 51,143-acre Humboldt Redwoods State Park; the best way to see them is to drive the 33-mile Avenue of the Giants that winds along the banks of the Eel River. The Eel River area is a popular place for swimming, fishing, rafting, camping, hiking and trail riding. Redwoods were felled by the lumber industry until the 1920's when the Pacific Lumber Company protected thousands of acres from the sawmill; the land was later purchased by a preservation society. A museum in the park highlights timber production and reforestation projects, and there is a self-guided tour of the world's largest redwood sawmill. Located 45 miles south of Eureka via Hwy. 101.

2 NAPA VALLEY

The fertile Napa Valley has been famous for its wine ever since Franciscan monks planted European vine cuttings in the region during the late 18th century. By 1880, the town of Napa had became the regional processing and shipping center for the fledgling wineries of the area. Today, the valley boasts more than 200 wineries, most of them located along the Silverado Trail and Hwy. 29, which traverse the 28-mile-long valley. Napa Valley's four main towns— Napa, Yountville, St. Helena and Calistoga—are located along these two routes. Many of the wineries offer regularly scheduled tours that take visitors through the wine-making process from beginning to end, and allow them to sample the wines. Located 45 miles northeast of San Francisco and 50 miles southwest of Sacramento.

3 FORT ROSS

Named *Rossiya* by the Russians, Fort Ross was built in 1812 by the Russian-American Company of Alaska so that they could enter the sea otter trade. The outpost also served as a wheat supply depot for the Russian settlements in Alaska. The only original building still standing is Rotchev House, the home of the last commander; the rest of the buildings are reconstructions of the originals. There is a reproduction of an 1826 Russian Orthodox chapel, seven-sided and eight-sided blockhouses and the officers' barracks. Each of the buildings is furnished as it would have been during the 30 years of Russian possession. A visitor center outside the stockade wall contains a historical display on Fort Ross and the Ranch Period—after the Russians left. Located 12 miles north of Jenner on Hwy. 1.

4 POINT REYES NATIONAL SEASHORE

According to local legend, this 73,000-acre peninsula of secluded beaches, rocky cliffs, grassy bluffs and forest sheltered Sir Francis Drake in 1579. The beach where he supposedly made repairs to his ship is named in his honor. Drake called the area Nova Albion (New England) probably because he felt it resembled the Dover coast. The 1870 Point Reyes Lighthouse warns passing ships away from the fog-covered rocky cliffs. Further inland, visitors can tour a reconstructed Miwok Indian Village; the Miwok were the first inhabitants of the peninsula. Visitors can walk along the Earthquake Trail that follows a section of the San Andreas fault line. Point Reyes, established as a National Seashore in 1962 and designated an International Biosphere Reserve by the United Nations 22 years later, protects a wide variety of wildlife—deer, elk, seals, whales, offshore sea lions and bird colonies. Located on Bear Valley Road, off Hwy. 1.

5 EUREKA

Founded in 1850 during a short-lived gold rush, Eureka eventually grew and prospered because of the lumber industry, not gold mining. The Old Town district preserves more than 100 Victorian homes, wood-frame warehouses, brick office buildings and clapboard shops. The Eureka Maritime Museum has exhibits on ship building, and a 1912 bank building houses the Clarke Memorial Museum, which specializes in Victorian artifacts, textiles, furniture and weapons. Fort Humboldt State Historic Park contains the ruins of a fort built in 1854 as well as a redwood-frame hospital from the mid-1800's. Located north of San Francisco on Hwy. 101.

6 LUTHER BURBANK GARDENS, SANTA ROSA

Horticulturist Luther Burbank, famous for developing the spineless cactus, was lured to California in 1875 by its rich soil and moderate climate. Arriving with a few Burbank potatoes, he bred and introduced new plant species—including 113 new varieties of plums and prunes. His modified Greek Revival home, greenhouse and two-acre memorial garden have been restored to resemble the originals. The Carriage House contains a horticulture museum that highlights Burbank's life and work. Located at the intersection of Santa Rosa and Sonoma Avenues in Santa Rosa.

7 ANDERSON MARSH STATE HISTORIC PARK

This park is named for Scottish immigrant John Anderson, who bought land in the area in 1885 and began to raise cattle. His old ranch house, built of hardy redwood, still stands. Visitors can tour the homestead. The marshland borders the Audubon Society's McVicar Preserve; it is the wintering ground for the American bald eagle, and the home and nursery of countless water birds, fish and other animals. The park also protects the archeological sites of more than 50 Indian villages, some of which are more than 10,000 years old. Located between Lower Lake and Clear Lake on Hwy. 53.

The varieties of grapes, especially Cabernet Sauvignon, that grow in the Napa Valley produce world-class wines. Many of the wineries, including the Barrel Room at Stag's Leap Vineyard, below, are open to visitors.

Boxley Valley, Newton County, Arkansas.

The Black Belt of central Alabama is a 25-mile-wide strip of rolling prairie land, connecting the northern and southern extremes of the Gulf Coastal Plain. The region gets its name from its rich, black soil, ideal for growing cotton; by the early 19th century, the state's economy depended on cotton. Cotton fields spawned prosperous plantations and wealthy planters built magnificent homes. Towns soon grew up around them—Selma, Eutaw, Demopolis and Greensboro.

During the Civil War, the earth was soaked red as it became a battleground. Mansions were burned to the ground by Union troops, or converted into hospitals. The war shattered the slave system upon which the cotton industry depended and boll weevil attacks on the cotton plants forced agricultural diversification.

HAUNTED MANSIONS

The towns of the Black Belt are proud of their historic past. Selma is believed to stand on the site of the ancient Indian village Piachee, where Chief Tuskaloosa met with Spanish explorer Hernando de Soto. Prior to the Civil War, the town was the center of the plantation aristocracy, and some of the classic plantation homes built during this period are open to the public. Sturdivant Hall's neoclassical architecture epitomizes the grandeur of these elegant homes. Grace Hall, another antebellum treasure, boasts a New Orleans-style gallery and courtyard, and a walled colonial garden. Alabama's mansions are no strangers to ghosts. Selma's Tale-Tellin' Festival every October allows local storytellers to bring out their best haunted house stories.

Demopolis was settled by a band of exiles from Napoleon Bonaparte's army. One of the town's highlights is Gaineswood, a 20-room Greek Revival mansion, fabled for its galleried rooms, glass ceiling domes with friezes and medallions, and its ghost. The plaintive strains of a flutina, a small, mid-19th-century accordion, sometimes echo through the halls. Greensboro's antebellum gems include the Noel-Ramsey House and Magnolia Grove, the 1840 Greek Revival

mansion in which the Spanish-American war hero Rear Admiral Richmond Pearson Hobson was born. Eutaw boasts over 30 antebellum structures, and its Black Belt Folk Roots Festival each August is a celebration of regional music, crafts and lore.

But the region's history goes back much further than the heyday of the cotton plantations. Moundville Archeological Park contains 20 mounds built by the Mississippians, called the Mound Builders, who lived in the region between A.D. 1050 and 1540. Their settlement of 3,000 people was the largest in the Southeast until it was abandoned more than four centuries ago. One of the flat-top earthen mounds is 58 feet tall and has a base that covers 1¼ acres. Visitors can tour a reconstructed Native American village with burial grounds, and a museum that displays objects found on the site. Brierfield Ironworks Park encompasses the ruins of the Bibb Furnace, where iron was smelted during the Civil War. Today it is a year-round locale for bluegrass and gospel festivals, Civil War reenactments and muzzleloading rifle competitions. Nature trails in the Talladega National Forest give visitors a chance to learn about the ecology of a bottomland hardwood area and the waterfowl of the Payne Lake wetlands.

FOR MORE INFORMATION:

Alabama Bureau of Tourism and Travel, P.O. Box 4927, Montgomery, AL 36103. (334) 242-4169 or (800) 252-2262.

The Civil Rights march from Selma to Montgomery started at Brown Chapel A.M.I. Church in Selma. A memorial bust of Dr. Martin Luther King, Jr., stands in front of the church.

Marble mantels, marble-tiled floors, ornate ceiling moldings, wall frescoes and period furnishings set off the interior of Sturdivant Hall in Selma.

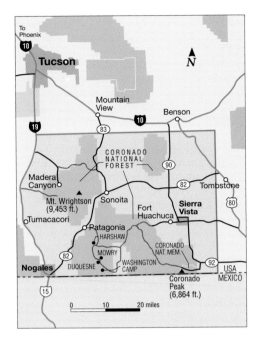

ising like mirages here and there from the Arizona desert are "sky islands": mountain ranges surrounded by the sizzling sands and spiny saguaros of the lowlands. A prime cluster of sky islands thrusts from a chunk of southeast Arizona centered around Patagonia, most of it within the Coronado National Forest. This enclave of conifer groves, singing creeks and lush canyons serves as a cool haven for a few human residents and lots of plant and animal inhabitants—and for travelers who know to seek its sanctuary.

Madera Canyon is an appealing place in which to make the acquaintance of the Sonoran Desert's sky islands. Visitors can park their cars at about 5,000 feet amid oak woodlands and walk upwards along a splashing stream bordered by flashy yellow columbines and white-barked Arizona sycamores. Hardy hikers can proceed on up past limber pine and aspen trees to the 9,453-foot peak of Mt. Wrightson, where 360-degree views reveal the Sea of Cortez 150 miles to the southwest and the San Francisco Peaks 250 miles to the north.

FOLLOWING THE BIRDS

Madera Canyon and many of the sky islands are renowned birding sites. One species prized by birdwatchers is the elegant trogan, a tropical beauty. The male shimmers in a coat of iridescent red, black, green and copper, and the female looks like a winged watercolor, all pink, white, tan and gray.

It pays to follow the birds, for they seem to know all the best places. Sonoita Creek Sanctuary, for example, attracts birders from all over the world, but its delectable meadows and huge cottonwoods invite leisurely strolls, as well. And birders go to Ramsey Canyon to see the hummers—14 different species of hummingbirds have been spotted there—but it's hard to imagine a finer place for a picnic than this green creek corridor.

Though the birds came to this area first, humans have been here a long time, too. Apaches and other Native American tribes used to roam the region. Europeans arrived in 1540, when the Spanish explorer Coronado crossed into what is now the U.S. at the site of the 5,000-acre Coronado National Memorial. The views from the parking lot at Montezuma Pass are notable, but travelers willing to labor up the steep, half-mile trail to the top of Coronado Peak will be rewarded with spectacular vistas of the desert, stretching far into Mexico.

Those interested in more recent history should drop by Fort Huachuca, a National Historic Landmark. It was soldiers from here who tracked down Geronimo. The fort's museum displays military artifacts in a turn-of-the-century building that used to be the bachelor officers' quarters.

The area's many ghost towns also speak of the frontier past. Slow but scenic forest service roads lead to abandoned villages such as Harshaw, Duquesne, Washington Camp and Mowry. A hundred mines producing silver, lead and zinc used to keep Mowry busy, but now only adobe ruins and an overgrown cemetery remain.

As motorists meander along the national forest roads, they'll see evidence that the present isn't too different from the past in these parts. Ranches still dot the region and on occasion cowboys sitting tall in the saddle can be seen loping across a distant ridge in search of stray cattle. Guest ranches and riding stables allow travelers to mount up and get a taste of life on the range. The cowboys' legendary love of horses is celebrated at Patagonia's Museum of the Horse, whose collection includes antique spurs, saddles, stagecoaches and paintings by famed western artists Frederic Remington and Charles M. Russell—all depicting horses, of course.

One booted foot in the past; working cowboys and spirited horses galloping across verdant valleys; murmuring springs ringed with wildflowers; skyscraping Douglas firs—truly, this is a land apart, a hideaway high above the desert, an island in the sky.

FOR MORE INFORMATION:

Tucson Convention and Visitors Bureau, 130 S. Scott Avenue, Tucson, AZ 85701. (602) 624-1817 or (800) 638-8350.

The Tumacacori Mission was built in 1691 by a Jesuit missionary and explorer. The ruins of the small church and its bell tower still stand.

Open oak-grass savanna flourishes southwest of the Huachuca Mountains, part of the Coronado National Forest.

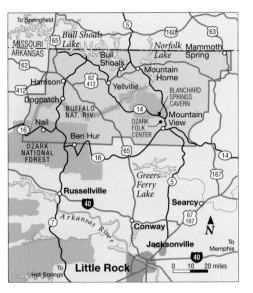

The craftsman's art is alive and well in the Ozarks, as these handmade fiddles attest. The isolation of the Ozarks region helped its inhabitants to preserve folk songs, stories and crafts that are fast disappearing elsewhere.

When God made the Ozarks, he peopled them with a folk prone to whimsy and showered the land with hidden geological surprises. The region has tiny towns grandly named Eros, Ben Hur and Parthenon, and others whimsically called Snowball, Dogpatch, Flippin, Morning Star and Yellville (home of an annual wild turkey calling contest).

Many of the geological wonders of this mountainous lake-fed region are underground. The Ozarks boast one of the ten largest caverns in North America, as well as Mammoth Spring, one of the world's largest springs. Within the Ozark National Forest, the Blanchard Springs Cavern has been called one of the greatest cave finds of the century. Its two trails, The Dripstone and The Discovery, wind through some of the largest cave rooms in the U.S., shimmering with giant flowstones, delicate rimstone and colorful stalactites.

Above ground the scenery is equally spectacular. The forest-clad Ozark Mountains are the only highland area between the Appalachians and the Rockies. Buffalo Canyon's 600-foot limestone cliffs and bluffs line the channel of the Buffalo National River. The river's aquamarine waters flow eastward from the Ozarks to the White River for 132 miles, making it great both for whitewater canoeing in spring and for rubber rafting during the summer.

North of the lush Ozark National Forest, only 10 miles separate the twin lakes of

The Buffalo National River's high limestone cliffs provide a steep impression for canoeists. The river is one of the few free-running, unpolluted rivers remaining in the contiguous United States.

Norfork and Bull Shoals. Together, these two bodies of water embrace 67,500 acres and 2,000 miles of shoreline. At Bull Shoals State Park winter birdwatching is at its peak in January, with eagle-watching cruises, waterfowl tours and live raptor demonstrations. The nearby Mountain Village 1890 is a restored 19th-century settlement. A trail from Mountain Village leads to the 350-million-year-old Bull Shoals Caverns, once inhabited by prehistoric peoples.

MOUNTAIN HERITAGE

Northern Arkansas is steeped in Ozark culture, with festivals featuring everything from beans to outhouse races. The zany

Dogpatch USA, a hillbilly theme park, is peopled with characters from the Li'l Abner cartoon strip. The Ozark Folk Center State Park, the only state park in the nation devoted to mountain folkways, depicts the Ozark way of life from 1820 to 1920. The park's 60 buildings are consecrated to Ozark traditional music and dance, storytelling and lore, cooking and 20 different crafts. In cabins built of local cedar and stone, artisans fashion brooms and white oak baskets, spin and weave, and make guns and fiddles. Visitors can sample fried pies filled with apples and peaches.

Music occupies a special place in Ozark life, and the Ozark Folk Center jumps with Ozark music of the 1800's and early 1900's. At weekly group sing-alongs from April to October, local musicians perform with fiddles, mountain dulcimers, spoons and banjos. The Ozark region also hosts a number of major musical festivals each year, including the Arkansas State Fiddler's Jamboree, the Arkansas Folk Festival and the Arkansas Bluegrass Festival.

State Highway 7, from Harrison down to Hot Springs, is considered to be one of the country's 10 most scenic highways. However, a detour down any number of side roads will be greeted by the evening song of the bobwhite and the whippoorwill, resinous piney air, flowering dogwoods and red buds, flea markets with country fiddlers and colorful quilts flapping in a playful breeze.

FOR MORE INFORMATION:
Arkansas Department of Parks and Tourism, 1 Capitol Mall, Little Rock, AR 72201. (501) 682-7777 or (800) 643-8383.

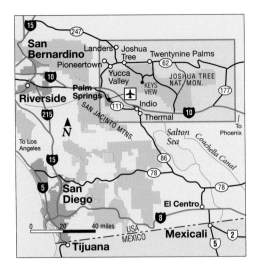

Across the Coachella Valley from Joshua Tree National Monument, the ranks of the San Jacinto Mountains rise up to greet the morning sun.

When Californians refer to "the desert," they usually mean the artificial oases of Palm Springs and its vicinity. But Palm Springs and its well-heeled brethren keep the real desert at arm's length. To sample its untamed counterpart, travelers should head east and north to Joshua Tree National Monument and the little communities that border it.

Out among the barrel cacti and creosote bushes of the Mojave Desert lie towns with names like Twentynine Palms, Thermal and Yucca Valley—towns that blend into the arid landscape. Earth and sand tones characterize the houses, and residents prefer native plants to grass. Desert dwellers have a bit of desert rat in them, as evidenced by the area's idiosyncratic events, such as Grubstakes Day, the Outhouse Races and Indio's National Date Festival. Even when it's not festival time, visitors to Indio can relax in date gardens and sip a date shake.

Wandering through these little desert communities always seems to turn up something interesting, as a jaunt on Highway 62 through Morongo Basin demonstrates. Near the hamlet of Joshua Tree lies the Joshua Tree and Southern Railroad Museum, packed with train paraphernalia. The whole town of Pioneertown was built in the 1940's as a movie set for Roy Rogers and Gene Autry.

THE WILD DESERT

When travelers are ready for the wild desert, they should venture into Joshua Tree National Monument's half million acres, a starkly beautiful land of monumental bronzed boulders, tough plants, furtive wildlife, and wide-open spaces.

The western half of Joshua Tree National Monument lies in the Mojave Desert. The plant that gave the monument its name flourishes in the high, cool Mojave. Known by their gray trunks, beckoning arms and spiky leaves, these desert monarchs are actually a species of yucca. The Joshua tree stores water in its trunk, and can grow as tall as 40 feet. Because the trees have no rings, their age cannot be accurately determined, but biologists reckon some specimens to be as old as 800 years.

Towering above the Joshua trees are a jumble of dramatic rock formations—one of the monument's biggest draws, and not just because of their striking appearance: Joshua Tree is a magnet for rock climbers. Particularly popular is a maze called the Wonderland of Rocks, where expert climbers inch up sheer rock faces.

Not far from the Wonderland of Rocks lies the Desert Queen Ranch, the home of local cattleman and prospector Bill Keys from 1917 until 1969. The main house, the dam, the corrals, the machine shop, the schoolhouse he built for his five children—all are still standing, mute testimony of the isolation of desert life and the independence it demanded.

The eastern half of the Joshua Tree National Monument is in the Colorado Desert. Low-growing creosote bushes replace Joshua trees as the dominant plant, and fewer mountains and rock formations interrupt the vast flatlands. This is even harsher desert, home to rattlesnakes, tarantulas and scorpions. But visitors are as likely to spot bighorn sheep, bouncy kangaroo rats and dainty kit foxes.

A fitting place to end a visit to the southern California desert is at Keys View, a 5,185-foot overlook near the southwest boundary of the monument. Perched up in the desert mountains, with the coyotes howling and the breeze whispering, it's clear there's a lot beyond the hotel pool.

FOR MORE INFORMATION:
Superintendent, Joshua Tree National Monument, 74485 National Monument Drive, Twentynine Palms, CA 92277. (619) 367-7511.

The Joshua tree is really a very large yucca, and can grow to 40 feet in height.

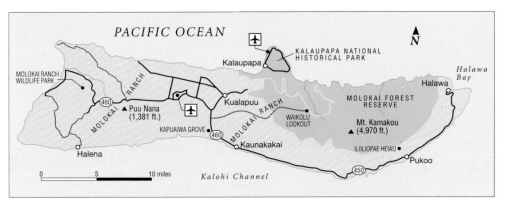

The Kapuaiwa Coconut Grove overlooks the beaches of Kilowea Beach Park. Molokai is Hawaii's fifth largest island.

Nearly forty miles long and only ten miles wide, Molokai has just about everything a tropical island needs. Wide, golden beaches skirt its western shore, royal palms and mangoes fringe the southern coast, and the evening sun casts its twin volcanic peaks into fine dramatic profile. The islanders are friendly, wildlife is abundant. There are sand dunes, coral reefs, hiking trails, waterfalls, grasslands, a rain forest, several historic sites, and a massive wall of jungle-covered *pali*, or sea cliffs, that qualifies as the world's tallest.

A single paved road runs the length of the island. The main settlement, Kaunakakai, has no traffic, no movie theater and no stoplights. By law, no building can exceed 30 feet. The coconut palms grow higher.

ANCIENT SHRINES

Even in ancient times, Molokai was a place of relative isolation. By the time the first inhabitants arrived, around A.D. 750, the rest of the Hawaiian chain had already been settled. The newcomers gained a reputation as powerful sorcerers. They built the great Iliiliopae shrine, rumor said, in a single miraculous night. (The shrine's massive foundation of surf-polished beach boulders

can still be seen.) Their royal fish ponds— tidal pools enclosed by stone breakwaters— still festoon the south coast. According to legend, they were the first Hawaiians to dance the hula, after the goddess Laka appeared on the summit of Puu Nana, the westernmost volcanic cone, to teach them how. Neighboring islanders left them alone.

Huge plantations covered much of Molokai in recent years. Sugar was the first cash crop; the R.W. Meyer Sugar Mill, built in 1878, has been restored and is open to visitors. Next came pineapples, with cattle-raising a major occupation as well. The 50,000-acre Molokai Ranch covers vast stretches of arid, prairie-like grassland in the island's western half. During local festivals such as Aloha Week (usually held in early October), Molokai cowhands stage an informal, Polynesian-style rodeo.

Wild game teems in these western prairies, most of it imported years ago by the Molokai Ranch: ring-necked pheasant, Barbary sheep, Indian black buck and more. There are axis deer from Asia, descendants of a herd given more than a century ago by a Japanese emperor to Hawaii's King Kamehameha V. More recent arrivals inhabit the 1,000-acre

Molokai Ranch Wildlife Park: giraffe, zebra, kudu, eland and other exotics graze in a landscape of thorn scrub and arroyo.

A different ecology pervades Molokai's eastern half, dominated by the 4,970-foot-high extinct volcanic peak of Mt. Kamakou. Here rainfall pours down at a rate of some 200 inches a year, cascades into precipitous valleys and feeds lush jungle growth filled with hundreds of rare bird species.

Molokai's most dramatic and most isolated site is a barren slab of stony land that juts out from the north-coast sea cliffs: the Kalaupapa National Historical Park. A sense of terrible mystery clings to it, of past heartbreak and eventual human triumph. Here, beginning in 1866, Hawaii confined its lepers. Those afflicted were brought by ship and abandoned, forced to fend for themselves until the disease consumed them. In 1873 a Belgian missionary, Father Damien, arrived to tend them. Damien himself died a leper—he is remembered as Hawaii's greatest hero—but the colony continued well into this century.

FOR MORE INFORMATION:
Hawaii Visitors Bureau, 2270 Kalakaua Avenue, Suite 801, Honolulu, HI 96815. (808) 923-1811

Molokai's natural beauty ranges from sandy beaches to mountains and valleys of lush tropical vegetation, seen here from Waikolu Lookout.

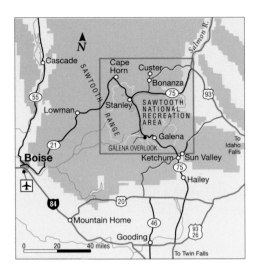

Captured at sunrise, with the Sawtooth Mountains as a backdrop, the Salmon River displays little of the fierce power that led explorers Lewis and Clark to call it "the river of no return."

Gazing out over central Idaho from the 8,701-foot Galena Overlook, it's easy to see why the mountain range to the northwest was dubbed the Sawtooths. If a child were handed a box of crayons and asked to draw mountains, he or she would produce an improbably jagged series of snow-topped saw teeth that would look just like this range. But the view from the overlook doesn't end with the Sawtooths. To the east and north lie the White Cloud-Boulder Mountains, less dramatic than the Sawtooths but actually higher. And between the ranges lies the achingly pretty Sawtooth Valley, which follows the gentle curves of the Salmon River. Creeks and lakes—more than 1,000 of them— sparkle throughout the valley and the mountains. Sagebrush spiced with wildflowers coats the valley bottoms; cottonwood, alder and aspen line the banks of the streams; and the mountainsides are cloaked by thick stands of lodgepole pines, Douglas firs and limber pines. It's little wonder that most of this gorgeous landscape was protected as the Sawtooth National Recreation Area in 1972.

People can enjoy this area in a multitude of ways, but the old standbys of driving and hiking work just fine. The main road, Highway 75, is the officially designated Sawtooth Scenic Route, and it doesn't disappoint. The route hugs the Salmon River, giving sharp-eyed visitors a chance to spot pronghorn antelope and mule deer in the flats, as well as the ospreys and bald eagles that feed in the river. The Indian Riffles overlook provides interpretive signs and an excellent view of salmon spawning beds. Motorists who want to branch off onto little-traveled byways have plenty of choice: Nip and Tuck Road affords spectacular views of the Sawtooths and skirts meadows alight with marsh marigolds and butter-

cups. People who do not mind bumping along at low speed can venture far back into the White Clouds on rutted dirt tracks with names like Pole Creek Road and Fourth of July Creek Road.

Even more opportunities exist for hikers. Understandably popular trails edge around the recreation area's five largest lakes, all of which back up against the eastern flanks of the Sawtooth Mountains—seemingly placed so visitors can exhaust their film shooting the reflections of the peaks on the still blue waters. The hundreds of smaller lakes that dot the high country also are popular, though they demand more from hikers. Up in these meadows and conifer forests, travelers might see elk, mountain goats, bighorn sheep, or cuddly little pikas and marmots squeaking from their rock piles. Some of the choicest trails crisscross the 217,088-acre Sawtooth Wilderness, which is largely the province of avid backpackers. But day hikers can nibble at the edges of this wild beauty via moderate routes, such as the Farley Lake and Hell Roaring Lake Trails.

GOLD RUSH RELICS
Civilization takes a back seat to the scenery in the Sawtooths, but the human touch is still evident. Just north of the recreation area, travelers can explore the ghost towns of Custer and Bonanza, magnets for thousands of gold seekers in the late 1800's.

These settlements comprise an Idaho State Centennial Park and include a mining museum and a historic gold dredge. Backcountry travelers will often stumble upon evidence of the gold rush, such as long-abandoned mining camps or overgrown equipment.

As the gold and silver played out, so did most of the fortune-hunters. Today the human presence is limited to a smattering of cabins, lodges and ranches. There is one notable exception: Stanley, the valley's metropolis. With a population of 71, Stanley is blessed with dirt streets, log houses, good restaurants, fine and funky lodgings, a rip-roaring saloon and famously laid-back residents, all amid a matchless natural setting. However, note that Stanley doesn't have a one-room schoolhouse. There are two rooms—but the high schoolers do have to go to Challis, 65 miles away. However, living in the shadow of the Sawtooths turns such hardships into mere inconveniences.

FOR MORE INFORMATION:
Sawtooth National Recreation Area, Star Route, Ketchum, ID 83340. (208) 726-7672.

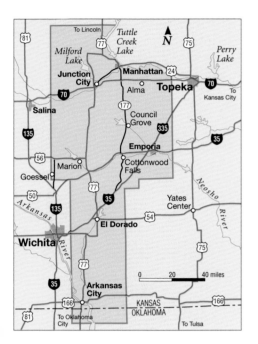

On a ranch near Alma, southeast of Manhattan, stockmen round up cattle grazed on the nutritious grasses of the Flint Hills. This upland area has provided prime grazing ever since settlers moved into the region.

A journey through the Flint Hills evokes the near-mystic experience of the early settlers as they discovered this land on their trek across the Great Plains 150 years ago. Native bluestem grasses still swathe the land as far as the eye can see. During the summer, a dazzling array of wildflowers contend for position amongst the tall grasses, adding brilliant splashes of color to a panorama that is already breathtaking. When the wind blows across the untamed prairie, the 20th-century traveler can still sense the spirit of the forgotten tribes and the wagon trains heading west.

Spanning a vast chunk of eastern Kansas, from close to the Nebraska border down to Oklahoma, the Flint Hills encompass five million acres of native tall grass prairie— the largest expanse in North America. Two million years ago, limestone sediment and thin layers of flint were deposited by the inland seas which covered the continental interior. Gradually, erosion carved out the landscape, from gentle hills and dales around Council Grove to the high, craggy escarpment of Chase County. For thousands of years, these rolling hills provided rich hunting grounds for nomadic groups such as the Kansa and Pawnee Indians. The introduction of the horse in the 16th century led to bison hunting.

BLUESTEM BOUNTY

Most settlers thought the flinty soil unsuitable for farming. A few built farmsteads in sheltered valleys close to water. As a result, the Flint Hills remained virtually untouched by the plow. Nowadays, the region's nutritious bluestem grasses make it prime ranching territory and an idyllic habitat for pronghorn, prairie chickens, white-tailed deer and wild turkeys.

Reminders of the Flint Hills' more recent history are to be found primarily in the center of the region. In 1826, after negotiations held at Council Grove on the Neosho River, the Osage Indians agreed to allow the Santa Fe Trail to run through their lands. Soon this spot became a favorite watering hole for trappers, traders, settlers and Indians. Council Grove's 12 national registered historic sites include Hays House, which has operated as a restaurant on the Santa Fe Trail since 1857.

Cottonwood Falls, in Chase County, features the Ronigher Museum, with one of the nation's largest collections of Indian artifacts. The elegant Chase County Courthouse has been astounding visitors since it opened its doors in 1873. Built from native limestone, in the Second Empire style, the building's interior also boasts a magnificent black walnut staircase.

On the outskirts of Manhattan, Fort Riley was originally built to protect settlers on the Santa Fe Trail. Home to the U.S. Cavalry for almost a century, the aura of its military beginnings is still pervasive. A tour of Custer House Quarters focuses on military family life and the fort's early history.

Explorations of the Flint Hills will lead to many delightful discoveries: the Mennonite Heritage Village in Goessel portrays Mennonite life of a hundred years ago; the restored period homes in Emporia were built by Welsh settlers. In Marion County, on the western edge of the Flint Hills, the lovely old stone dwellings built by settlers in the 1860's are now home to skilled artisans.

The Flint Hills affect all who pass through. This landscape has inspired many painters and poets over the years. Nature lovers exult in its abundant wildlife, and sightseers simply revel in the majestic vistas.

FOR MORE INFORMATION:

Travel and Tourism Division, Kansas Dept. of Commerce, 700 S.W. Harrison, Suite 1300, Topeka, KS 66603. (913) 296-2009 or (800) 2-KANSAS.

At the foot of the Flint Hills, the wheatfields of central Kansas stretch into the distance. Beginning in the 1870's, Mennonite farmers from Russia pioneered the cultivation of wheat on these plains.

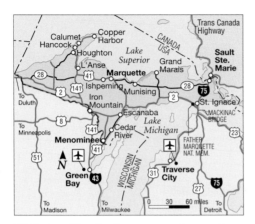

Fringed by shadowy green pines and ghostly white birches, Michigan's Upper Peninsula is a nine-million-acre forest bounded by Lake Superior, Lake Michigan, Lake Huron and the neighboring state of Wisconsin. Its vital statistics are impressive. It is 384 miles long and 233 miles wide—larger than the states of Massachusetts, Rhode Island, Connecticut and Delaware combined.

The Upper Peninsula is a paradise of peaks and valleys, and boasts 4,300 inland lakes, more than 150 waterfalls, thousands of miles of meandering rivers and perfect trout fishing streams. It offers plenty of opportunities for summertime berrypicking, or gazing at autumn's colors. The town of Paradise, located on Whitefish Bay, lures visitors with its sandy beaches and miles of hiking trails. Fishing is also great in the nearby Tahquamenon River.

A wintry, windswept Upper Peninsula means snow: 200 to 300 inches or more of the powdery white stuff each year. The breath-snatching downhill runs of the Porcupine Mountains and the 12-story-high ski jump at Pine Mountain attract thrillseekers, while cross-country skiers favor silent trails deep inside the Sylvania Wilderness and Recreation Area.

SAULT SAINTE MARIE

One of the best places to get a bird's-eye view of the peninsula is from the 21-story Tower of History in Sault Sainte Marie. The tower also overlooks the massive Soo Locks, which link the Upper Peninsula with Canada. Monster floodgates accommodate Great Lakes super-freighters up to 1,000 feet long. It takes only a few minutes for 10 million gallons of rushing water to raise or lower vessels to the next stage in the system.

In the 1600's, travelers didn't have it so easy. Canoes carried the first French trappers and missionaries across the choppy Straits of Mackinac to the Lower Peninsula. These early visitors were forced to portage around Sault Sainte Marie, or the Falls of St. Mary, which drop about 21 feet from Lake Superior into Lake Huron. In 1668 Jesuit priest Jacques Marquette founded a mission here, making Sault Sainte Marie the oldest permanently inhabited town in the state. There is a two-hour boat trip through the locks and the visitor center in Fountain Park displays a working model of the locks.

Miner's Castle, a weathered sandstone pinnacle, is one of the formations in Pictured Rocks National Lakeshore on Lake Superior.

The Peninsula can also brag about another feat of engineering. Mackinac Bridge, dubbed Mighty Mac by locals, joins the Upper Peninsula to Lower Michigan. The five-mile-long suspension bridge is used by more than 6,000 cars a day. Erected in 1957, it weighs more than a million tons, equivalent to 4,444 Statues of Liberty.

While priests came to save souls, later arrivals stampeded in with dreams of wealth. Loggers harvested the lofty white pines, and zealous miners tackled the vast copper and iron deposits. Although logging is still a viable industry, the played-out mine shafts are darkened. (During the 19th century, about 90 percent of copper mined in the U.S. came from the Peninsula.)

Visitors can tour some of the mines including the Iron Mountain Iron Mine, in operation from 1877 to 1945. Trains go through 2,600 feet of tunnels and caverns, and guides describe early mining methods. At the Iron Ore Museum, near Caspian, visitors can tour a pioneer mining village.

FOR MORE INFORMATION:
Upper Peninsula Travel & Recreation Association, Box 400, Iron Mountain, MI 49801. (906)774-5480 or (800) 562-7134.

Tahquamenon Falls State Park is nestled among the forested shores of Lake Superior in Whitefish Bay. The tea-colored water of the Lower Falls is caused by the leaching of surrounding tamarack.

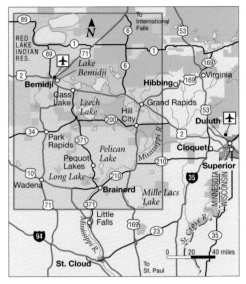

The cry of the wolf is sometimes heard in the inner reaches of the Lake Country's aspen, white birch and maple forests. Other large mammals in the region include moose and black bear.

Minnesota's automobile license plates proclaim the state to be the "Land of 10,000 Lakes." Seen from the air, the heart of central Minnesota is indeed lake-strewn, with almost more water than land. From Mille Lacs Lake, 90 miles north of the Twin Cities, to Lake Bemidji, up the trail another 120 miles, they glint in the sun. Forests of pine, birch and maple trees fill in the wide, open spaces between them.

For the Ojibwe, this was Minsisagaigon—"everywhere lakes." The lakes are for the most part shallow, water-filled depressions that were left behind by glaciers during the Ice Ages. Central Minnesota is a watershed feeding the Mississippi and Hudson Rivers and Lake Superior drainage basins.

From tiny beaver ponds to massive sheets of water like Mille Lacs (18 miles wide by 14 miles long, but only 40 feet deep), there is certainly enough water here to keep anglers smiling. Sport fishing is a prime recreational activity in this region, with walleye, crappies, perch and bass the main prizes. The elusive muskie is the subject of many rueful one-that-got-away stories. Forty-mile-wide Leech Lake, named by the Ojibwe for a legendary giant leech, hosts the International Eelpout Festival each February. Thousands of fishermen head onto the ice-covered lake to try to snag the lowly eelpout, a cross between a snake and a catfish, known locally as the world's ugliest fish.

Numerous fishing camps and resorts dot the shores of many of the lakes. These hideaways are perfectly suited to a lazy

Clear, unclouded waters and pristine forests are two reasons the Lake Country is such a popular vacation destination. Mille Lacs Lake, right, is the region's largest lake.

summer lifestyle. Many lakes have beaches, ideal for swimmers and shoreline walkers. With so many lakes to choose from, canoeing is a natural in these parts.

BUNYAN COUNTRY
Following on the heels of the fur traders, loggers opened up the lake country during the 19th century. They took advantage of the region's vast stands of white pine, floating their bounty to market. This is still Paul Bunyan Country. Statues of the giant logger and Babe, his big blue ox, stand tall in Bemidji, along the shore of Lake Bemidji. The town and the lake were named after

Bay-may-ji-ga-maug, an Ojibwe chief whose name meant "A Lake With Cross-Waters" because the Mississippi River cuts across one corner of the lake there.

In the old days, loggers felled trees indiscriminately. Today, Minnesota's trees are a renewable resource with 14.8 million acres of timber available for harvest, much of it in these lake lands. However, state forests such as Hill River, Emily, Land O'Lakes, Golden Anniversary and Pillsbury, as well as the Chippewa National Forest, promise plenty of stillness and solitude for hikers and campers. Moose, black bears and even wolves inhabit the inner forestland.

The headwaters of the Mississippi rise in Itasca State Park, a few miles southwest of Bemidji. From a birthplace that is easy to step across, the Mississippi swells to almost 100 feet in width by the time it cuts through downtown Grand Rapids.

Part of an old school in Grand Rapids has been turned into a museum in honor of local-girl-turned-movie-star Judy Garland. Of course, there is a yellow brick road on the grounds. A Judy Garland Festival is held in June on her birthday weekend each year.

FOR MORE INFORMATION:
Minnesota Office of Tourism, 100 Metro Square, 121 7th Place East, St. Paul, MN 55101. (800) 657-3700 (U.S.), (800) 766-8687 (Canada) or (612) 296-5029.

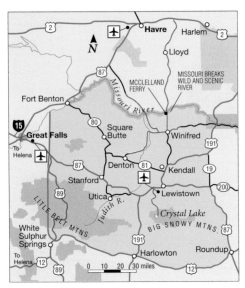

Lewistown lies nestled amidst the mountain ranges of the Snowies, the Judiths and the Moccasins. The town survives today because it is a center for ranching in the region.

Many people who have never been to Montana's Judith Basin have seen it before—on the canvases of cowboy artist Charles Marion Russell. The rolling, grassy hills, the barrel-chested buttes and the infinity of the prairie form the background for many of his paintings. It was here in the basin that the 16-year-old Russell got his first job; he herded sheep on the Judith River and lost the whole flock. Russell's first Montana hometown was tiny Utica, where some of his work hangs today. Russell painted the area masterfully, but the Judith Basin looks even better in person.

The basin comprises the expanse of central Montana drained by the Judith River, a tributary of the Missouri. The area got its name in 1805, when Captain William Clark named the river after his cousin (whom he would later marry). However, it was not until the late 1800's that ranchers and farmers began settling the basin, a process that accelerated rapidly after the discovery of gold and silver.

TRANSITION ZONE

The basin lies in a transition zone between the Rockies and the Great Plains, and it looks like a blend of both. Scattered mountain ranges bulge above the prairie, but they consist of rounded mountains cloaked by forests, not jutting, rocky peaks.

The northern edge of the Judith Basin is dominated by the Missouri River. This stretch of the mighty river is classified as "wild and scenic," and it's just that as it flows through the rugged badlands of the Missouri Breaks and past the striking White Cliffs. A number of ferries span the river; the old-fashioned McClelland Ferry carries a maximum of three cars at a time across the river on flat-bottomed boats hauled by cables.

The Judith Basin's close connection with the frontier era is readily apparent in Lewistown, the region's commercial center. The town can boast of four historic districts. Of particular interest is the Silk Stocking District, containing the homes of some of Lewistown's wealthiest pioneer-era citizens. The town's annual Cowboy Poetry Gathering underscores the frontier influence. There are even bison in town, though they're kept in a fenced pasture at the headquarters of the C.M. Russell National Wildlife Refuge.

Montana's gold and silver strikes brought fortunes for some and disappointment for many more. The remains of some of the Judith Basin's long-abandoned mining towns can be visited, including the old town of Kendall, 20 miles north of Lewistown, where visitors can see the ruins of a church, a bank, a general store, and some of the mines. The Kendall Mine still produces some 50,000 ounces of gold a year. Free

Fields of wheat flourish in the prairieland, located north of Lewistown.

summer tours show visitors how gold mining has changed since the days when prospectors panned the basin's creeks.

In the Little Belt Mountains during the late 1800's, miners kept finding little blue stones in their sluiceboxes. For years they ignored them. Finally, in 1894, a prospector sent some to Tiffany and Co. in New York for appraisal and was astonished when he was told that he had found "sapphires of unusual quality." Called "Yogo sapphires" because they were discovered in Yogo Gulch, these gems are renowned for their clarity and brilliance. Yogo sapphires can be seen on the engagement ring given to England's Queen Elizabeth by Prince Philip—but it's easier to get a good look at them at some of the stores in Lewistown.

Travelers seeking an overview of the Judith Basin head to the Big Snowy Mountains, a 100,000-acre mountain island amid the grasslands. Hikers ascend through conifer forests, past chokecherry bushes, and across mountain-goat territory to Grandview Point. Somehow it's no surprise that the point is very near the geographical center of the Big Sky state. Gazing down on the prairie and rivers and hills is like contemplating a huge Charles Russell painting—only better.

FOR MORE INFORMATION:
Lewistown Chamber of Commerce, Box 818, Lewistown, MT 59457. (406) 538-5436; or Travel Montana, P.O. Box 20533, Helena, MT 59620. (404) 444-2654 or (800) 541-1447.

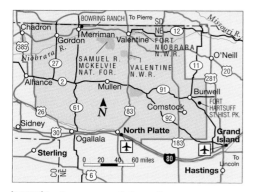

The largest sand dune formation in the Western Hemisphere extends over 18,000 square miles deep into the heart of Nebraska. The wind-rippled prairie grasses of the Sand Hills—Indian grass, big and little bluestem, prairie sand reed and sand lovegrass—protect these undulating dunes.

Six ecological systems mix and mingle along the fast-running Niobrara River. The river's steep canyons, rimmed with birch, oak and pine trees, host a biological crossroads. Leftovers of Ice-Age fauna and flora still live in the cool wet canyons that feed into the Niobrara River. In one stretch, 30 miles east of Valentine, there is a unique coalition of plants and animals. Paper birch and ponderosa pines, desert cactus and prairie grassland share the same terrain, thousands of miles from their regular habitat. The Sand Hills is also renowned for its

countless natural lakes. A high water table provides underground irrigation and succulent nourishment for the prairie grasses. A cattleman's paradise, the Sand Hills is home to more cattle than folks, averaging one person per square mile in some areas.

CALL OF THE WILD

The call of the wild is strong. In Valentine National Wildlife Refuge more than 300,000 waterfowl and shore birds haunt the 70,000 acres of shallow lakes and marshland, from blue-winged teal to mallards, pintails to ruddy ducks. Every spring and fall, sandhill cranes issue their musical call as they fill the skies in V-shaped formations. Buffalo herds still roam the open prairie at Fort Niobrara National Wildlife Refuge, although they share the vast space with antelope, elk, deer and Texas longhorns, descendants of the herds driven north from Texas a century ago. Grouse reside in the peaceful pines of Samuel R. McKelvie National Forest, while bald and golden eagles take advantage of the updrafts along the Niobrara River in search of winter sustenance. Fishing opportunities abound at Merritt, Calamus and Sherman Reservoirs, where the waters teem with catfish, walleye and crappie.

Thousands of years ago, the region was the home of buffalo, elk, deer, antelope and wolves. Then the Indians came in search of the buffalo and finally, not so long ago,

The grassy dunes of the Sand Hills are often likened to a sea of grass. The region is dotted with working cattle ranches.

homesteaders moved into the area. The military played an important peacekeeping role between the local Indians and the early settlers. Fort Hartsuff was built near Burwell in 1874, only to be abandoned six years later once its mission was completed. It is now reconstructed as a typical infantry outpost of the 1870's, with guides in period dress to draw visitors back to the past.

Gordon, in Sheridan County, is said to typify the Old West. The history of the area and its people won international renown through a series of books written by a local writer, Marie Sandoz—a much respected chronicler of the Old West. Self-driving tours of Marie Sandoz country bring her stories vividly to life.

Nebraska's only living history ranch has been preserved at the Arthur Bowring Sand Hills Ranch Historical Park, near Merriman. The cattle ranch still operates as it did at the turn of the century. In marked contrast to the ranch house are the intriguingly named "Nebraska marble" homes. They are actually made from sod and were erected by ingenious and practical homesteaders between 1860 and 1900. A few sod houses have survived, such as Dowse Sod House, near Comstock.

A drive along Highway 2 provides an overall perspective of a land where ranches are measured in miles, where prairie fields seem to cover the universe, and where our pioneering days do not seem so far away.

FOR MORE INFORMATION:
Nebraska Tourism, P.O. Box 94666, Lincoln, NE 68509-4666. (402) 471-3796 or (800) 228-4307.

The Niobrara River provides great outdoor activities for fishermen and canoers. Placid in some places and fast in others, the river is considered to be one of the top 10 canoeing rivers in the U.S.

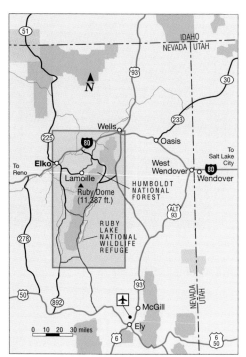

Elko's Commercial Hotel was the first in the state to offer both entertainment and gambling.

The Rubies surprise people. Most of the travelers humming along Highway 80 through northeastern Nevada expect a monotonous diet of sagebrush grassland—not 11,000-foot mountains. Even old Nevada hands are surprised, because the Rubies are unlike any of the other 150 mountain ranges in the state.

Elko is the gateway to the Rubies, which dominate the horizon to the south and east. A hard-working town, Elko is a center for the ranching and mining industries. Typical events include the rodeo, the Western Folklife Center's Cowboy Poetry Gathering, and the Cowboy Music Gathering.

WESTERN HERITAGE

Many of Elko's institutions also reveal its rapport with the countryside. The Northeastern Nevada Museum covers the ranching, mining and natural history of the region. The Western Folklife Center saves and promotes cowboy poetry, music and crafts, such as horsehair braiding. Though technically not an institution, J.M. Capriola Co. & Garcia Bit and Spur has been outfitting working cowboys since 1929, and handcrafted Garcia saddles have prevented saddle sores on people from Will Rogers to Sylvester Stallone.

Visitors to Elko can enjoy the area's rich Basque heritage at places like the Star Hotel, located in an old wooden boarding house that has been an off-season home to Basque sheepherders since 1910. Meals are served family style and include authentic Basque dishes. Every Fourth of July weekend, Basques from around the world gather for the National Basque Festival, featuring *irrintzi*, or yelling contests, Basque dancing, and traditional sporting competitions. Most grueling is the Basque pentathlon, which includes events such as hauling a half-ton concrete block 120 feet.

For a closer look at the Rubies, travelers can take a route that circumnavigates all but the southern tip of this 10-by-60 mile, north-south range. Along the way they'll encounter some beautiful agricultural valleys and a couple of minuscule towns, most notably Lamoille, with its charming Little Church of the Crossroads and its incongruous heli-skiing operation. Ruby Lake National Wildlife Refuge teems with ducks, geese, cranes, eagles, herons and some rare trumpeter swans.

Several side roads lead into the Rubies from the main circle route, but none can compare with Lamoille Canyon Road, a 12-mile Forest Service byway that slithers into the heart of the mountains. The walls of this spectacular glacial canyon rise as much as 2,500 feet above the road, prompting visitors to gaze upward at hanging valleys and avalanche scars and beyond the canyon rim to ice fields and waterfalls.

After lingering at a number of picnic sites, campgrounds and interpretive turnouts, motorists reach the end of the road. But it's hardly the end of the line. Trails invite you to stroll through lowland meadows alive with lupine, fireweed and larkspur, or spend a week above the timberline along the 43-mile Ruby Crest Trail. A compromise would be to hike a couple of miles up the crest trail. Up there it can snow in the summer while Elko swelters in the heat.

At these heights, the characteristics that separate the Rubies from other Nevada ranges become clear. Ample moisture has created an unusual number of lakes and has fostered the growth of the largest area of alpine tundra in the Great Basin. The Rubies also were the most glaciated range in the basin, and they have the cirques, moraines and U-shaped canyons to prove it. Even though the stones after which the Rubies were named turned out to be garnets, the range deserves its name anyway, because it's a gem.

FOR MORE INFORMATION:

Nevada Commission on Tourism, Capitol Complex, Carson City, NV 89710. (702) 687-4322 or (800) 638-2328.

The snowcapped Ruby Mountains receive as much precipitation as the Rockies and the Sierras. They are the wettest mountains in the state.

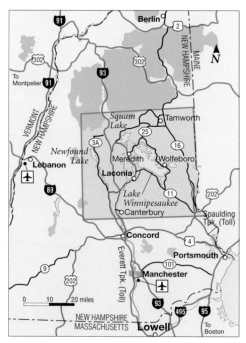

The summit of Rattlesnake Mountain offers a sweeping view of Squam Lake. This watery jewel, sometimes known as "Golden Pond," is the second largest lake in New Hampshire.

When the colonial governor of New Hampshire decided to build a summer home, he picked a spot on the eastern shore of sparkling Lake Winnipesaukee. The neighborhood was then, as it is today, a marvel of quiet forests, ethereal views, and a near-perfect summer climate. The governor clearly knew what he was doing, even if no one else had done it before. In that year of 1769, Governor John Wentworth may have founded the first summer resort in America.

Such, at least, is the claim of the citizens of Wolfeboro, where they proudly point out the massive granite foundations of the governor's lakeside getaway. It burned down in 1820. Many other cottages would spring up to follow it along 72-square-mile Winnipesaukee's 182-mile shoreline, or on its 274 habitable islands. But seen from the water—especially from the decks of the century-old cruise ship *Mount Washington*—Winnipesaukee still seems mostly wilderness.

This respectful partnership with nature emerges throughout the Granite State's Lakes Region, which begins at the Maine border and spreads west, covering much of central New Hampshire just south of the White Mountains. The entire region measures about 50 by 50 miles, and Winnipesaukee, directly in the center, is its dominant natural feature. Yet the lake is only one of some 273 lakes and ponds in the region. Squam Lake, Little Squam, Winnisquam, and Newfound Lake are among the other stars in this shimmering galaxy of clean, unclouded waters. Squam may be the most famous—if by another

name. The 1981 Henry Fonda-Katharine Hepburn movie, *On Golden Pond*, was filmed on its peaceful shores.

AUTHENTIC TOWNS
The towns of the Lakes Region glow with all the authentic patina of New England. Wolfeboro, whose compact center is directly on the Winnipesaukee shore, manages to preserve its look of yesterday while serving as a hub for cross-country skiing, bicycling, scuba diving and fishing. Farther afield are such ancient and appealing towns as Tamworth, home of the Barnstormers, the state's oldest professional theater, and Center Sandwich, site of one of New Hampshire's biggest country fairs. Sandwich is also a noted stronghold of high-grade craftsmen, whose art, textiles and ceramics are sold in the shop of Sandwich Home Industries, overlooking the town green.

Across Winnipesaukee, Meredith is a former mill town that has successfully reincarnated itself as a shopping and water sports center. The town's unique asset is a big millrace that splashes through the heart of town and plunges in a dramatic waterfall at the lakeshore. At Weirs Beach, a traditional waterfront boardwalk has all the lively trimmings: penny arcades, pizza and ice cream shops, and bumper cars. Its harbor is home port for the venerable *Mount Washington*.

One-of-a-kind sites abound in the Lakes Region. Perched on a mountaintop

near Moultonborough overlooking Winnipesaukee, Castle in the Clouds is the dream house of an early-1900's shoe tycoon; today the 5,200-acre estate is a family recreation area popular with horseback riders and hikers. The Science Center of New Hampshire, surrounded by woods and meadows in Holderness on Squam Lake, is devoted to the state's wild animals, many of them brought there injured and nursed back to health. South of Laconia is the Canterbury Shaker Village, a museum community of 23 original structures, which recalls the Shakers' simple elegance and their quest for righteousness.

The New Hampshire Farm Museum, in Milton, demonstrates the colorful, if granite-hard, existence of vanished rural generations. In such places, the history, culture and natural beauty of New Hampshire come together in an extraordinary whole— a view polished by time and enhanced by the region's glittering lakes. Governor Wentworth, the first summer person, must be pleased.

FOR MORE INFORMATION:
Lakes Region Association, P.O. Box 589, Center Harbor, NH 03226. (603) 253-8555 or (800) 60-LAKES; or New Hampshire Office of Travel and Tourism, P.O. Box 856, Concord, NH 03302.

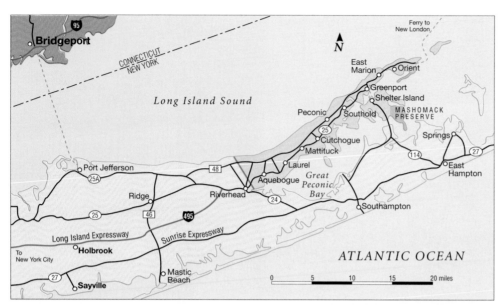

The Regina Maris, *a three-masted barquentine built in 1908, lies moored at the town pier in Greenport. The schooner is being restored.*

A peaceful world of old fishing villages, pristine beaches and sylvan landscapes can be found a mere 70 miles east of New York City. A tour of Long Island's 28-mile-long North Fork may well end with a carload of freshly picked fruits and vegetables, samples from award-winning wineries, and a new appreciation of early colonial life.

Long Island's eastern tip is divided into two forks, North and South, split by the Great Peconic Bay. The route to the North Fork lies at the end of the Long Island Expressway, beyond Riverhead, via County Road 48 and Route 25.

Benefiting from rich glacial soils and moderate sea breezes, this emerging wine region has already earned much acclaim. Most of North Fork's 12 wineries offer tours and tastings. Green "Wine Trail" signs along Routes 25 and 48 (parallel highways running the length of North Fork) direct passersby to the wineries. The wineries are especially a pleasure to visit in late September and October.

Some of America's oldest settlements are found along North Fork. Explorations may commence two miles east of Palmer Vineyards, on Route 48, at Hallockville Museum Farm in Aquebogue. Four generations of the farming Hallock family lived until recently in this 18th-century homestead, which has been restored to reflect a typical North Fork farm of the late 1800's.

Route 25 passes through one delightful village after another, beginning at Laurel, where the superb views over the Great Peconic Bay are ample reason for there to be so many sea captains' homes here, mainly built in the early 19th century.

Farther along, villages like Mattituck—with its 18th-century homes, a Presbyterian

Church built in 1715 and a rare Octagon House—or Cutchogue, where the Village Green is bordered by the oldest English-style houses in New York State, deserve some time. Southold, named after an English village in Suffolk, was settled in 1640. Almost every building has a tale to tell, but particularly the nine historic buildings in the Southold Historical Society's Museum Park.

In the former whaling center of Greenport, the whaling captains' handsome homes with their widow's walks are mostly tucked away down the town's narrow side streets. When the whaling boom ended in the mid-nineteenth century, the town turned to more traditional fishing, and continued shipbuilding. Currently docked in Greenport Harbor, the *Regina Maris*—a wooden barquentine built in 1908—is being prepared to serve as an oceanographic research vessel.

Near the end of Route 25, the village of Orient was designated a Historic District in 1976. Its streets are lined with gracious

Palmer Vineyards in Aquebogue is just one of the many North Fork vineyards, all of which are open to the public.

old homes, and the Oysterponds Historical Society has recreated life in the 17th, 18th and early 19th centuries in a compound of historic buildings.

Harvest season on North Fork yields its own riches. Roadside stands laden with Long Island potatoes, cauliflower, broccoli and a wide variety of fruits beckon city shoppers, and "pick your own" enthusiasts can literally have a field day.

A seven-minute ferry ride connects Greenport to Shelter Island, where miles of serene white beaches, sailboats bobbing in Dering Harbor and old-fashioned stores all amplify the island's faraway feel. Within the Nature Conservancy's 2,200-acre Mashomack Preserve, visitors can bike or hike along numerous trails.

Every spring, fall and winter, birders head down to North Fork to glimpse the many uncommon birds on their migratory flights.

FOR MORE INFORMATION:

Long Island Convention & Visitors Bureau, Eisenhower Park, 1899 Hempstead Turnpike, Suite 500, East Meadow, NY 11554. (516) 794-4222 or (800) 441-4601; Southold Town Promotion Committee, P.O. Box 1865, Greenport, Long Island, NY 11971. (516) 765-2588; Shelter Island Chamber of Commerce, Box 598, Shelter Island, NY 11964. (516) 749-0399.

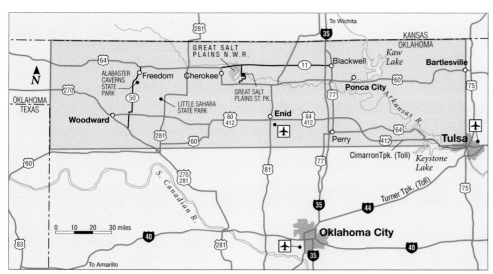

The Marland Mansion in Ponca City was built in 1928 by oil baron E.W. Marland. The 55-room Italian Renaissance-style palace bears the inscription "A man's home is his castle."

The Cherokee Outlet's arresting landscape of sweeping prairieland, sand dunes, mesas and buttes extends for more than 200 miles in an east-west direction across the top of Oklahoma. When the Cherokee were relocated to Oklahoma (then called the Indian Territory) by the federal government in the 1840's, they were given the northeastern corner of the state as their homeland. To provide hunting grounds, the government allowed them access to an additional seven million acres of game-rich land, known as the Outlet. (The Outlet is sometimes referred to by its nickname—the Strip.)

Following the Civil War, cattlemen discovered the region's excellent prairie grasses as they drove herds of Texas longhorns through Oklahoma to railheads in Kansas. The Cherokee leased a part of their western land in the Outlet to cattle ranchers. This in turn sparked land-hungry homesteaders to pressure the government to make the fertile farmland available for settling. Finally in 1891, the Cherokee agreed to sell a parcel to the federal government for $8.5 million.

LAND RUNS

When the government announced that the land was to be opened up to settlers, it set up five land runs to ensure that everyone had an equal chance. The largest took place in September 1893, when more than 100,000 people tore through northern Oklahoma, eager to snap up one of the 40,000 land lots. Within hours, 6.5 million acres had been "settled," and towns seemed to spring up overnight. By the end of the 19th century, the Outlet had entered its golden era as part of the Midwest's wheat boom. Farming, ranching and petroleum fueled the activities of all who lived here.

Today, more than 67 Native American tribes call Oklahoma home. The Plains Indians and Pioneer Museum in Woodward and the Museum of the Cherokee Outlet in Enid focus on their culture. Blackwell and Perry both have Museums of the Cherokee Strip; Ponca City's Pioneer Woman Statue and Museum pays homage to the women who settled the West.

The town of Cherokee is the gateway to the 10,000 acres of the Great Salt Plains National Wildlife Refuge and Great Salt Plains Lake. Visitors dig for selenite crystals, located just beneath the surface of the enormous flats. More than 250 species of birds take temporary refuge here, including the endangered whooping crane. Little Sahara State Park is a 1,500-acre region of sand dunes formed by ancient river deposits. The vast cave at Alabaster Caverns, near Freedom, is the world's largest gypsum cave. The caverns contain formations of alabaster and selenite crystals in a kaleidoscope of pinks, whites, rusts and grays.

FOR MORE INFORMATION:

Oklahoma Tourism and Recreation Department, 2401 N. Lincoln Blvd., Suite 500, Oklahoma City, OK 73150. (800) 652-6552.

The Plains Indians and Pioneers Museum in Woodward presents the history of the Native Americans and cattle ranchers who settled in the region. Displays include murals and exhibits of Indian relics.

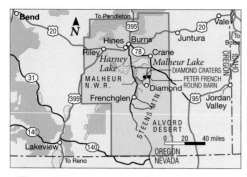

The Alvord Desert is a playa—a dry lakebed of alkali, blinding white in color and virtually devoid of vegetation.

S outheast Oregon seems to belong in another state. Instead of the sweeping beaches and rain-drenched forests that most people associate with Oregon, the southeast quadrant serves up the high desert: sagebrush grasslands, brawny red-rock buttes and endless wide open spaces—plus some incongruous surprises.

Harney County south of Highway 20 constitutes the heart of Oregon's undiscovered corner. This sparsely settled area is bigger than Vermont but has a population of only 7,000 people. In the town of Crane, students from isolated ranches and settlements attend the only public boarding high school left in America. Many of the towns only come to life on Saturday nights.

Travelers who yearn to gaze upon so much elbow room need only head for the Steens Mountain. Volcanic activity shouldered the 30-mile-long Steens high above the neighboring flats, creating the largest fault block on the continent. Eons later, glaciers carved the rock into dramatic shapes and left behind glittering lakes.

A 66-mile loop road, designated as a Back Country Byway by the Bureau of Land Management (BLM), winds up the Steens, tightropes along its crest, and then eases back down to the desert floor. The road begins in sagebrush grassland, climbs into pinyon-juniper woods, ascends into the aspens, and finally winds through a treeless alpine zone near the 9,773-foot summit. Along the way, visitors should keep an eye out for elk, deer, marmots and coyotes, as well as pronghorn antelopes—among North America's fastest mammals. Once at the crest, wildlife watchers can scan the steep terrain for bighorn sheep or check the thermals for golden eagles and prairie falcons. Most people, however, simply can't take their eyes off the view.

It is worth driving around the mountain to explore the flatlands a mile below the summit. Here, the eerily beautiful Alvord Desert awaits. Framing the Alvord Desert are sand dunes, salt desert scrublands and mountains in all directions.

MARSHY MALHEUR

Thirty miles and a world away from the Alvord Desert is Malheur National Wildlife Refuge. Snowmelt from the surrounding mountains collects in the Malheur-Harney Basin, creating a 185,000-acre oasis of lakes, marshes and wet meadows. Seeking refuge from the high desert, animals congregate in Malheur, making it outstanding for wildlife viewing. Visitors may see beavers, badgers, minks, pygmy rabbits, muskrats, bobcats or any of the other 52 species of mammals recorded at the refuge. But what visitors usually come for is the birds.

During the spring and fall migrations, Malheur is like a vast, open-air aviary. The refuge teems with some 260 species of birds, including avocets, herons, ibis, loons, ospreys and white pelicans. Thousands of ducks and geese alight on lakes and ponds. Mallards, Canada geese and regal sandhill cranes flock to the grain fields of nearby Blitzen Valley to feed.

From Malheur another BLM Back Country Byway, the Diamond Loop, leads northeast back into the desert. Motorists may be astonished to see wild horses racing alongside the road. These are the Kiger mustangs, almost-pure descendants of horses originally brought over by the Spanish. The loop also passes the Peter French Round Barn, a relic of French's 19th-century cattle empire. The barn is 100 feet in diameter, 35 feet high, and has a 60-foot lava rock corral inside. It was used to break horses during the winter.

The highlight of the byway is Diamond Crater, site of a big lava flow 25,000 years ago. Its lava cones, fissures, cinder pits and other volcanic features remain relatively unweathered. Amid such dramatic evidence of the Earth's primordial processes, there is a potent sense of southeast Oregon's elemental nature.

FOR MORE INFORMATION:
Tourism Division, Oregon Economic Development Department, 775 Summer St. N.E., Salem, OR 97310. (503) 986-0000 or (800) 233-3306.

Desert paintbrush and sagebrush grow in the foothills of the Steens Mountain. The vegetation changes from grassland to a treeless alpine zone near the 9,773-foot summit.

T he pastoral vistas of Bucks County bring rural England to mind: winding country lanes, babbling brooks, rich green forests, gentle hills and valleys dotted with old fieldstone farmhouses. Named after England's Buckinghamshire, the county lies nestled in the Delaware River Valley between the cities of Philadelphia and New York. During the 18th and 19th centuries, a major stagecoach route connecting these two cities cut through the heart of the county, and country inns quickly sprang up to serve the stagecoach passengers; one of the earliest inns dates to the 1680's, and 30 of them date to pre-Revolutionary days.

By the 1780's, the area had become a fashionable vacation spot for ladies and gentlemen who needed a revitalizing dose of country air. The town of Bristol, located in the southern part of the county, boasted a very stylish spa which was visited by prominent members of society. Bucks County continues its long tradition of

The cozy pastoral scenes of Bucks County are an inspiration to visitors who want to unwind. The same serene landscape inspired painters from the Delaware Valley who flocked to the region in the early part of this century.

welcoming inns and warm hospitality, and is still a perfect place for weekend retreats and holidays.

REVOLUTIONARY LEGACY

For military buffs, the county offers an insight into the nation's revolutionary heritage. On a frigid Christmas Day in 1776, General George Washington led his rebel forces across the icy Delaware River to successfully defeat the Hessian troops in Trenton. Washington Crossing Historic Park commemorates this event. Every year on Christmas Day, reenactments of the famous 1776 crossing take place in the park. Bowman's Hill Tower, a hilltop lookout during the American Revolution, provides a bird's-eye view of the county. Nearby, visitors can stroll through the 100-acre Bowman's Hill Wildflower Preserve, which shows off native plants from Pennsylvania. The David Library of the American Revolution houses a collection of more than 6,000 volumes on the War of Independence, as well as 2,500 original documents, mostly letters, written during the war.

Early colonial history comes to life at historic Fallsington, a 300-year-old Quaker village with more than 90 historic buildings dating from the 17th, 18th and 19th centuries. The English-style country estate of William Penn—a prominent Quaker as well as the founder of Pennsylvania—is located at Pennsbury Manor in Tullytown. Here, costumed guides carry on the day-to-day life of the 17th century with Quaker simplicity and grace, surrounded by some of the most outstanding 17th-century furniture in the U.S.

Pearl S. Buck's home at Green Hills Farm in Perkasie, near Dublin, is a 60-acre homestead that typifies the architecture of 19th-century Pennsylvania. The 158-year-old farmhouse, now a National Historic Landmark, contains many fine examples of Oriental and American art, as well as the writer's own memorabilia.

Henry Chapman Mercer is another local celebrity. Mercer, a rich architect, archeologist, potter and scholar, built three reinforced concrete structures in Doylestown. The Mercer Museum, a seven-story concrete building, houses some 40,000 pre-industrial American tools, as well as a large collection of ordinary objects. Mercer believed that much could be learned about a society by studying its everyday articles. The Fonthill Museum, Mercer's home, was modeled after a medieval castle and houses his vast collection of tiles from distant lands, including 4,000-year-old Assyrian clay vouchers. The Moravian Potters and

The grounds of Lentenboden—a private residence in New Hope—are open to the public. Early May is the best time to view the tulips.

Tile Works is a living history museum, where the tiles are still being produced using turn-of-the-century techniques.

The Delaware Canal, which begins at Easton and finishes at Bristol, is one of the few preserved canals in the country. Completed in 1832, the canal was soon a major transportation route; by the 1860's, more than 2,500 boats and barges pulled by mules were using the waterway. During the summer, sightseeing barges leave from the tiny village of New Hope, taking visitors along a two-mile stretch of the canal. But perhaps the true essence of Bucks County is to be found by following every beckoning detour and by soaking in the tranquil ambience of its gentle countryside.

FOR MORE INFORMATION:

Bucks County Tourist Commission, 152 Swamp Road, Doylestown, PA 18901-2451. (215) 345-4552 or (800) 836-2825.

The Caribbean island of Puerto Rico was discovered by Columbus in 1493, and was a Spanish colony until 1898, when the island was transferred to the United States. But on this densely populated island—the smallest of the Greater Antilles—history coexists happily with a natural environment of unsurpassed variety and lushness. Within a short drive from San Juan, the capital, visitors can sample some of the Caribbean's finest beaches or visit historic communities and picturesque fishing villages. In the interior rise the rugged Sierra de Luquillo Mountains, whose crowning glory is the 28,000-acre Caribbean National Forest—the only tropical rain forest within the U.S. National Forest system.

El Yunque Recreation Area is at the heart of the Caribbean National Forest's dense tangle of vines, giant ferns and towering palms. El Yunque—"the Anvil"— takes its name from the second-highest peak in the Sierra de Luquillo, whose form resembles a blacksmith's anvil. The preserve contains more varied flora per acre than any other U.S. National Forest—240 tree species, 20 species of epiphytes, and more than 50 varieties of ferns. Dozens of trails wind through the forest. Hikers might spot the endangered Puerto Rican parrot, a bright green bird with brilliant blue wings and a scarlet forehead. Fifty other species of birds, and millions of tiny, chirping tree frogs, called *coquís*, provide a dense forest song.

El Yunque was originally decreed a protected area by the Spanish crown in 1876. With such rich and diverse vegetation, and more than 300 different types of soil, the forest today serves as a laboratory for studies in rain forest management, and plays an important role in conservation.

There are four different rain forest zones. The most spectacular, the *tabonuco*, covers the lower slopes below 2,000 feet. The six-

mile El Toro trail leads hikers through the four rain forest levels, from the dramatic thickets of 30-foot-high tree ferns and giant palms draped with lianas and air plants, to the smaller palm forest at higher elevations, and the stunted dwarf vegetation growing on mountain ridges. This challenging trail leads to Pico El Yunque, the 3,532-foot rain forest summit, where lookout towers afford spectacular panoramic views.

COASTAL ENCOUNTERS

On the way to the national forest, a number of treats are in store. The coastal highway along the northern shore of the island takes in the Piñones Forest Reserve, near Loíza. Here, amid extensive coconut plantations, is Puerto Rico's largest coastal mangrove zone. Loíza itself is the site of San Patricio Church. Construction of the church began

A hiker, left, surveys the majesty of the Big Tree Trail, which winds through El Yunque's tabonuco (true rain forest), lowest of the park's four rain forest levels. The mist-covered high altitudes of El Yunque, shown above, are still virgin rain forest.

in 1645, and it is the oldest active parish church on the island.

At Río Grande, the road joins Highway 3, which loops around the island's eastern tip. The public beach at Luquillo is renowned as one of the world's most beautiful, and the town is a good place to explore the surrounding foothills. Farther east, the sailing and boating center of Fajardo lies at the base of Cape San Juan, site of the Cabeza San Juan Nature Reserve. The site centers around a restored lighthouse, built 1877-82.

A fascinating architectural curiosity can be seen at Humacao, a few miles to the south of the national forest. The Casa Roig was built in 1920 by architect Antonio Nechodoma for a prominent Humacao family. Employing the style of famed American architect Frank Lloyd Wright, Nechodoma adapted the design of the house to a tropical setting. The T-shaped building, with its airy balconies, has been restored as a cultural center and museum.

FOR MORE INFORMATION:

Puerto Rico Tourism Company, 575 Fifth Ave., 23rd Floor, New York, NY 10017. (800) 223-6530; Caribbean N.F., P.O. Box 25000, Río Piedras, PR 00928-2500. (809) 766-5335 or (800) 866-7827.

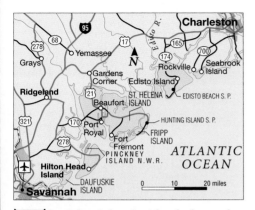

The Atlantic barrier islands that make up South Carolina's Sea Islands hug the coast between Charleston and Savannah, Georgia. The islands have been whipped by hurricanes, plundered by pirates, raided by the British Army and Union troops and exploited for cotton. Although some of them have been overbuilt with condominiums and hotels, a few are yet unspoiled. On these islands, sandy roads twist under brooding live oaks draped with eerie filigrees of bleaching moss. Sea oats and lanky palmettos sway in the breeze, bursts of wisteria and yellow jasmine festoon plantation mansions and tabby houses of crushed oyster shells. Turtles sun on beaches, wild boars roam the forest and shrimp boats bob on the horizon.

SEA ISLAND COTTON

Edisto is one of the islands that has been spared over-commercialization. In 1860, the island was one vast field growing Sea Island cotton—one of the finest cottons ever produced. This crop made the island one of the wealthiest agricultural communities in the world. Today, there are a few

antebellum homes and plantations still standing, reminders of the great wealth of this bygone era. Edisto Beach State Park's 1,225 acres protects a mile and a half of beach, an oak forest, open salt marshes and some of the tallest palmetto trees in South Carolina. Dolphins romp in the bay, and the tidal creeks contain shrimp, crabs, oysters and clams. The island is also a haven for deer, otter, raccoons, great blue herons, white egrets and osprey. Visitors can beach-comb for sand dollars, shells, fossils and relics of the Edisto Indians, whose ancient shell mounds dot the island. The Edisto River Canoe and Kayak Trail meanders along 56 miles of the scenic backwater river.

Hunting Island, tucked between Edisto Island and Daufuskie Island, is a popular state park. Located on the island's ocean-side is a three-mile-long beach of white sand; at low tide, the beach is a trove of shells and sand dollars. The island's 1,200-foot-long pier is the longest on the Atlantic coast, and fishermen are as likely to snag sharks and barracuda as smaller species of fish. Anyone with the stamina to climb the spiraling 181 steps to the top of the island's lighthouse, constructed in 1875, will be rewarded with a fine view of the island. The Light House Trail is an elevated boardwalk that winds through lagoons rich with trout, bass and whiting, and salt marshes where 250 species of birds can be observed.

In his novel *The Water Is Wide*, Pat Conroy writes of "the tide-eroded shores and the dark, threatening silences of the swamps in the heart of the island." He was describing Daufuskie—a five-mile-long, three-mile-wide Atlantic barrier island whose name means "Place of Blood." During the Civil War, Daufuskie and other

Rhett House, in the town of Beaufort on Port Royal Island, is one of its antebellum treasures. The mansion, which now operates as an inn, is a reminder of the Sea Islands' more prosperous days as a major cotton producer.

South Carolina Sea Islands were famous for their highly prized, long-fibered cotton. French silk mills bought crops even before they were planted. But after the war, plantation owners fled the islands, and only the descendants of their slaves stayed on, making a living from fishing and farming. Today, Daufuskie is accessible only by boat, and many of its 110 full-time residents still speak Gullah—a Creole language based on archaic English and a West African dialect.

FOR MORE INFORMATION:
South Carolina Lowcountry and Resort Islands Tourism Commission, P.O. Box 366, Hampton, SC 29924. (803) 943-9180; or South Carolina Department of Parks, Recreation and Tourism, 1205 Pendleton Street, Columbia, SC 29201. (803) 734-0235.

Signs of civilization are few and far between on some parts of Daufuskie Island. A narrow road of dirt and crushed shells is the only road on the island.

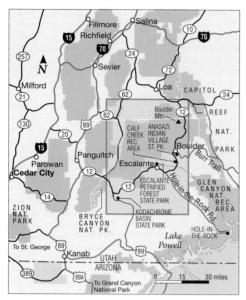

There is also a museum that houses pottery, arrow points and other items from the site.

A few miles south of the park lies the modern town of Boulder, where fewer people live than once lived at the Anasazi village. Boulder was one of the last communities in America to rely on pack trains. Vehicles couldn't get there until the Escalante River was finally bridged in 1935.

Another fine way to meet the desert is to hike to Lower Calf Creek Falls from the trailhead just a few minutes' drive from Boulder. The nearly flat path meanders for about three miles beneath high sandstone cliffs painted with desert varnish, passing beaver ponds, rock arches, 1,000-year-old petroglyphs and Anasazi ruins. The prizes at the end are a 126-foot waterfall, a cooling swim and a shady cottonwood grove.

ESCALANTE RIVER

Highway 12 crosses the Escalante River a few miles south. The Escalante was the last major river to be officially discovered in the lower 48 states, and its watershed remains an unmapped maze. Hikers who venture there are privy to radiant canyons of curvaceous, multicolored Navajo sandstone, hidden springs and caves sprinkled with Native American artifacts. Many of the same rewards can be had by stopping at viewpoints along Highway 12, by taking short walks from the highway and by plunging deep into Escalante canyon country via the historic Hole-in-the-Rock Road.

Mormon pioneers carved this rugged road out of the rock in 1879 when 236 settlers, hundreds of horses and more than 1,000 cattle set out from Escalante to colonize a site in southeastern Utah. The 290-mile journey took them six months. The road still gets pretty rough, and people driving cars might want to limit themselves to the 12-mile run from the highway out to Devils Garden. This garden grows hoodoos—weird, tilted sandstone spires.

Kodachrome Basin State Park offers brilliantly colored rock formations such as this spire, topped with a cap rock.

Five miles beyond the Hole-in-the-Rock Road turnoff, Highway 12 enters Escalante, population 650, plus lots of cows and chickens. It's the biggest town around and serves as the area's commercial center. Just south, travelers can amble through Escalante Petrified Forest State Park, where a nature trail leads to several outcrops of ancient petrified trees of beautifully patterned rock.

Another 30 miles down Highway 12 visitors reach the turnoff for Kodachrome Basin State Park, where they can explore on foot or by guided horseback, wagon and stagecoach rides. They also can camp in Kodachrome Basin, and some may choose to do so—the realm revealed is difficult to leave. In fact, when you come out of the Basin, you might just turn east and head back up Highway 12 to see how things look from the other direction.

FOR MORE INFORMATION:

Color Country Travel Region, P.O. Box 1550, St. George, UT 84771-1550. (801) 628-4171 or (800) 233-8824.

T here is a 100-mile stretch of Utah's Highway 12 that runs from Capitol Reef National Park to Bryce Canyon National Park. The highway traverses a wild, beautiful and mysterious landscape that harbors sidewalk-width sandstone canyons, 100-foot waterfalls, ancient native American ruins, colossal rock arches, dinosaur fossils, sun-dappled pine forests, and a sprinkling of civilization in the form of pioneer history and backwater towns.

In the north, Highway 12 starts just west of Capitol Reef and quickly rises to almost 9,000 feet, slipping through lake-dotted forests of ponderosa pine, aspen and fir. Looming Boulder Mountain dominates the view to the west, but travelers can gaze forever to the east, contemplating the canyon country of Capitol Reef and a huge expanse of fiery red-rock desert.

As the road begins its descent from the mountains, it passes Anasazi Indian Village State Park. About 900 years ago some 200 Anasazi lived here, and visitors can wander and wonder at the ruins of their town.

The Burr Trail crosses the Waterpocket Fold of Capitol Reef. In dry weather, the Trail is passable to cars driven by patient drivers. It is well worth sampling a few miles of its desert scenery.

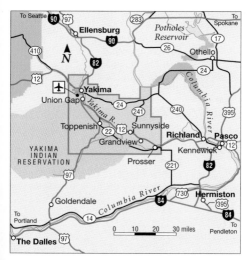

The rich volcanic soil and long summer days combine to make agriculture the main industry in the Yakima Valley. The region is the second largest producer of fine wine grapes in the United States.

V alley. The word suggests a place of refuge; a place blessed with sweet water, shady orchards and fields green with swaying grass; a place where neighbors sit on generous front porches shooting the breeze, and where—on Saturdays—the high school parking lot turns into a bustling farmers' market; in short, a place where the living is easy. The Yakima Valley is such a place.

But Yakima has more. Because the valley includes the prosperous city of Yakima, population 55,000, and because the local wine industry is thriving, it offers certain sophisticated virtues that purely bucolic valleys lack.

Most visitors arrive from the north on Highway 82 and begin their exploration in the city of Yakima. One of the most popular stops is North Front Street, a historic district that blends turn-of-the-century stone buildings with boutiques, restaurants, and a winery tasting room. On a hot summer day visitors and locals alike throng Grant's Pub Brewery for a Scottish Ale or an Imperial Stout—all the beers come from Yakima Brewing & Malting, the first brew pub in the United States. For a dose of undiluted past, visitors can walk or drive to the Yakima Valley Museum, which is famed for its horse-drawn vehicles—the largest collection west of the Mississippi.

The museum also contains some Native American artifacts, but travelers shouldn't content themselves with these displays when they can drive 18 miles south to Toppenish and experience a living Native American culture at the Yakima Indian Cultural Center. Pioneers came to these parts before the turn of the century; the Yakima Indians came here before the turn of the millennium. Located at the edge of the huge Yakima Reservation, which lies southeast of the valley, the center tells the Yakima story from their point of view.

Visitors to Toppenish also can't help but notice the town's famous murals. Monumental scenes from the area's past adorn the outside walls of many of Toppenish's buildings. Each year more are added, including one painted by a group of artists in about eight hours in the annual "Mural-in-a-day" event.

WINE COUNTRY

North, south and east from Toppenish sprawls the Yakima Valley wine country, where warm days, cool nights and rich soils are converted into prize-winning grapes and premium wines. Some two dozen wineries and their vineyards grace the valley. They range from little family operations such as Chinook Wines, which produces about 1,500 cases a year, to its Prosser neighbor, Hogue Cellars, which puts out about 100,000 cases a year and ships wine all around the globe. At harvest time in September dozens of barefoot teams from around the Northwest show up at the annual Grandview Grape Stomp to see who can most quickly stomp the most juice out of a vat of grapes. Though the wineries get the lion's share of attention, the agricultural bounty of the valley extends well beyond the vineyards.

Yakima County leads the nation in the production of apples, hops and mint; it's a top producer of peaches, pears, corn, cherries and apricots; and it grows some of just about everything else under the sun. Travelers poking along the backroads of the region, particularly the old valley highway, can feast their eyes on mile after mile of fertile fields and orchards. Those who want both a visual and a literal feast can take a basket of just-picked strawberries, a bottle of local wine, a wedge of cheese, a freshly baked loaf of bread, and sit down under a cottonwood tree overlooking the river. Isn't that what valleys are all about?

FOR MORE INFORMATION:
Yakima Valley Visitors and Convention Bureau, 10 North Eighth Street, Yakima, WA 98901. (509) 575-1300 or (800) 221-0751.

INDEX

PICTURE CREDITS

Cover photograph by Kunio Owaki/
The Stock Market

2 Tom Algire
5 Frank S. Balthis

NORTHEAST KINGDOM
8, 9 Paul O. Boisvert
10 Paul O. Boisvert
12 (upper) Paul O. Boisvert
12 (lower) Tom Algire
13 Alan L. Graham/f/Stop Pictures
14 Robert Holmes
15 (upper) Robert Holmes
15 (lower) Robert Holmes
16, 17 Bo Zaunders/The Stock Market
18 Clyde H. Smith/f/Stop Pictures
19 (upper) Clyde H. Smith/f/Stop Pictures
19 (lower) Courtesy Shelburne Museum

FINGER LAKES
20, 21 Kenneth Garrett
22 Nathan Benn/Woodfin
    Camp & Associates
24 Hardie Truesdale
24, 25 Kenneth Garrett
25 Andy Olenick
26 Nathan Benn/Woodfin
    Camp & Associates
26, 27 Kenneth Garrett
28 James Cavanaugh
29 (upper left) Michael Melford
29 (lower right) Clyde H. Smith/f/Stop
    Pictures

THE CHESAPEAKE
30, 31 David A. Harvey/Woodfin Camp
    & Associates
32 (upper left) Bill Field
32 (lower right) Ron Levine
34 (both) Heather R. Davidson
35 (upper) Kit Breen
35 (lower) Heather R. Davidson
36 (upper) Heather R. Davidson
36 (lower left) Frederick D. Atwood
37 Heather R. Davidson
38 Heather R. Davidson
39 (middle) Courtesy The Ward Museum
    of Wildfowl Art

39 (lower right) Heather R. Davidson
40 (upper left) Kenneth Garrett
40 (lower left) Stephanie Maze/Woodfin
    Camp & Associates
41 (lower left) Peter Gridley/Masterfile
41 (upper right) Kenneth Garrett

POTOMAC HIGHLAND
42, 43 Ron Snow
44 Stephen J. Shaluta, Jr.
46 (left) Stephen J. Shaluta, Jr.
46 (right) Arnout Hyde, Jr.
47 Stephen J. Shaluta, Jr.
48 (left) Ron Snow
48, 49 Stephen J. Shaluta, Jr.
49 (right) Ian Adams
50 Hardie Truesdale
51 (lower left) Stephen J. Shaluta, Jr.
51 (upper right) David Fattaleh, courtesy WV
    Division of Tourism & Parks

HIDDEN VALLEYS
52, 53 Dennis Nolan/R. Hamilton Smith
    Photography
54 Richard Hamilton Smith
56 (both) A.B. Sheldon
57 Larry Knutson
58 (upper left) Larry Knutson
58, 59 Richard Hamilton Smith
59 (right) Larry Knutson
60 (both) Balthazar Korab
61 (upper) Larry Knutson
61 (lower) Courtesy Vesterheim Norwegian-
    American Museum

CAJUN COUNTRY
64, 65 Philip Gould
64 Philip Gould
66 Philip Gould
66, 67 Les Riess
67 Philip Gould
68 Philip Gould
69 (both) Philip Gould
70 C.C. Lockwood
71 Philip Gould
72 Philip Gould
72, 73 C.C. Lockwood
73 C.C. Lockwood
74 (both) Philip Gould
75 (both) Philip Gould

TEXAS HILL COUNTRY
76, 77 Philip Gould
78 Ron Levine
79 Bob Daemmrich
80 (upper) Frank S. Balthis
80 (middle left) Steve Bentsen
80 (lower) Larry R. Ditto
81 Ron Levine
82 (left) Bob Daemmrich
82, 83 Bob Daemmrich
83 (right) Mills Tandy
84 Mills Tandy
85 (both) Frank S. Balthis

SAN JUAN SOJOURN
86, 87 Tom Algire
88 Tom Bean
90 (left) David Hiser/Photographers/Aspen
90 (right) Michael Collier
91 Frank S. Balthis
92 (upper) Tom Bean
92 (right) David Hiser/Photographers/Aspen
93 Tom Bean
94 (left) David Hiser/Photographers/Aspen
94 (right) Frank S. Balthis
95 Nicholas Devore III/Aspen Photographers
96 Tom Bean
97 (both) Tom Bean

THE WALLOWAS
98, 99 David Jensen
100 (upper left) Chuck Pefley/Frozen Images
100 (lower right) David Jensen
102 (both) David Jensen
103 (both) David Jensen
104, 105 (all) David Jensen
106 Rollin Geppert/Frozen Images
107 (upper left) Ric Ergenbright
107 (lower right) Steve Bly

MENDOCINO COUNTY
108, 109 Frank S. Balthis
110 Robert Holmes
112 Frank S. Balthis
112, 113 Frank S. Balthis
113 Robert Holmes
114 Frank S. Balthis
114, 115 Frank S. Balthis
116 (left) Mills Tandy
116 (upper) Frank S. Balthis

116, 117 Robert Holmes
118 (both) Robert Holmes
119 (both) Robert Holmes

GAZETTEER
120 Matt Bradley
121 (left) Jean Higgins/Unicorn Stock Photos
121 (right) Mike Clemmer/Stock South
122 (both) Tom Bean
123 (both) Matt Bradley
124 (lower left) Wayne Lynch/Masterfile
124 (upper right) Tim Fitzharris/Masterfile
125 (upper) Jeff Gnass/The Stock Market
125 (lower) Rita Ariyoshi
126 Rollin Geppert/Frozen Images
127 (lower left) Lowell Witcher/Unicorn
    Stock Photos
127 (upper right) Cotton Coulson/Woodfin
    Camp & Associates
128 (lower left) Denis MacDonald/Unicorn
    Stock Photos
128 (upper right) Hans Blohm/Masterfile
129 (upper) Erwin & Peggy Bauer/Natural
    Selection
129 (lower) Richard Hamilton Smith
130 (both) Larry Mayer
131 (both) Jodi Cobb/Woodfin Camp &
    Associates
132 (both) Jeff Mullins
133 William Roy/The Stock Market
134 (upper) Kenneth Winchester
134 (lower) Susan Farley/New York Newsday
135 (both) Fred W. Marvel, courtesy
    Oklahoma Tourism
136 (both) David Jensen
137 (lower left) Mike Dobel/Masterfile
137 (upper right) Jack Rosen
138 (upper right) J. Sapinsky/The Stock
    Market
138 (middle) Tom Bean
139 (lower) Karen Kasmauski/Woodfin Camp
    & Associates
139 (upper right) Ken Laffal
140 (both) Tom Bean
141 Sisse Brimberg/Woodfin Camp &
    Associates

Back cover photograph by Frank S. Balthis

ACKNOWLEDGMENTS

Lisa Beets, Manhattan Visitors Bureau; Susan Bladholm, Oregon Tourism Division; Bunny Breuer, Hidden Valleys Inc.; Kathleen Brown, Diversions; Cammie Conlon, Mendocino Coast Chamber of Commerce; Tyler Hardeman, Arkansas Dept. of Parks and Tourism; Stephanie Hughart, West Virginia Division of Tourism & Parks; Marlee Iverson and Victor Bjornberg, Montana Office of Tourism; Michael Kordos, Texas Tourism Bureau; Valerie Longevitsh, Long Island Convention and Visitors Bureau; John Middlebrook, Lake Willoughby Chamber of Commerce; Bruce Morgan, Louisiana Tourism; Pat Phillips, Cheryl O'Brien and Bob Kimmel, USGS; Barb Thompson, Yakima Valley VCB.

Cartography: Map resource base and shaded relief courtesy of the USGS; maps produced by Hatra Inc.

The editors would also like to thank the following: Alfredo Abeijon, Margaret Caldbick, Lorraine Doré, Irene Huang, Geneviève Monette, Tamiko Watanabe.